RISK ASSESSMENT AND MANAGEMENT

Fundamentals of Effective Risk Management

Dr Ian Messenger

Interior Design and Formatting: Nonon Tech & Design

ISBN: 978-1-7380088-0-3 (Paperback)
ISBN: 978-1-7380088-1-0 (Hardback)

Table of Contents

CHAPTER 1

Introduction to Risk Assessment and Management

I<small>N</small> today's dynamic and uncertain world, individuals, organizations, and society must be able to effectively manage and evaluate risks. Risks can originate from a variety of sources, including financial insecurity, operational difficulties, technological vulnerabilities, natural disasters, regulatory changes, and even unforeseen occurrences such as pandemics. In order to ensure the stability, sustainability, and success of businesses and projects, it is essential to have a thorough comprehension of risk assessment and risk management.

Risk assessment is the process of systematically identifying, analyzing, and evaluating potential threats to an organization or undertaking. It involves recognizing and comprehending the probability and impact of a variety of events or circumstances that could constitute a risk or an opportunity. By conducting a comprehensive risk assessment, individuals and organizations can proactively identify potential hazards, vulnerabilities, and weaknesses, allowing them to make informed decisions and implement the most effective strategies to mitigate or exploit these risks.

WHAT IS RISK?

Risk is the likelihood that an event or circumstance will occur and influence objectives, goals, or outcomes. It involves ambiguity and the possibility of both positive and negative outcomes. Risk is commonly defined in the context of risk management as the combination of an event's probability of occurring and its potential impact.

Risk can arise from a variety of sources and can be classified into various categories. Here are some frequent forms of danger:

FINANCIAL RISK

Financial risk is defined as the possibility of loss or uncertainty arising from financial transactions, investments, or operations. It includes a variety of elements that might have a detrimental impact on an individual's, organizations, or the general economy's financial health. Understanding financial risk is critical for making sound decisions and putting risk management strategies in place. Here are some specific financial risk examples:

MARKET RISK

Market risk occurs from financial market volatility, such as changes in interest rates, exchange rates, commodity prices, and stock market values. As an example:

INTEREST RATE RISK

If interest rates rise, a company that relies on short-term loans with variable interest rates may suffer higher borrowing costs.

CURRENCY RISK

An importer importing goods from another country bears the risk of currency depreciation, which can raise import costs.

EQUITY RISK

Investors in the stock market face the danger of share price drops, which can result in financial losses.

CREDIT RISK

Credit risk is the possible loss resulting from borrowers' or counterparties' failure to meet their financial obligations. Here are several examples:

DEFAULT RISK

A bank that makes loans has the danger of borrowers defaulting on their payments, which could result in financial losses.

COUNTERPARTY RISK

When financial institutions enter into derivative contracts, they run the risk that the counterparty will be unable to meet their contractual commitments.

LIQUIDITY RISK

Liquidity risk occurs when a business lacks adequate funds to meet its financial obligations or is unable to efficiently convert assets into cash without incurring a severe loss. As an example:

CASH FLOW RISK

A company that relies on a single major customer for revenue may experience liquidity problems if the customer fails to pay or goes bankrupt. Investors in illiquid assets, such as certain types of bonds or real estate, may find it difficult to sell those assets swiftly and at a fair price.

OPERATIONAL RISK

The potential loss caused by inadequate or failing internal processes, systems, or human behaviors is referred to as operational risk. Here are several examples:

FRAUD RISK

Organizations face the risk of financial loss as a result of fraudulent activity by workers or third-party vendors.

TECHNOLOGY RISK

A corporation that relies extensively on technology may suffer financial losses as a result of system breakdowns, cyber-attacks, or data breaches.

COMPLIANCE RISK

Noncompliance with laws, regulations, or industry standards creates compliance risk, which can result in financial penalties or legal consequences. As an example:

REGULATORY RISK

Financial institutions may risk fines or legal action if they violate anti-money laundering, consumer protection, or data privacy legislation.

COUNTRY/POLITICAL RISK

The potential financial losses caused by unpredictable political situations, changes in government policies, or economic instability in a specific country are referred to as country or political risk. Here are several examples:

SOVEREIGN RISK

Investors in government bonds bear the risk of the issuing country defaulting or restructuring its debt.

REGULATORY RISK

Businesses operating in nations with unpredictability or bad regulatory regimes may incur financial risks and constraints.

These examples demonstrate the wide range of financial dangers that individuals and businesses confront. Effective risk management is identifying, assessing, and executing risk-mitigation techniques to maintain financial stability and resilience in the face of unpredictability.

OPERATIONAL RISK

Operational risk refers to the potential for loss or damage resulting from insufficient or failed internal processes, people, systems, or external events. It incorporates a variety of risks associated with an organization's day-to-day operations. Contrary to financial and market risks, operational risks are not explicitly connected to financial transactions or market fluctuations. Human error, system malfunctions, legal and regulatory compliance issues, supply chain disruptions, and external threats are the primary causes of errors.

Operational risks can have significant repercussions for businesses, including financial losses, reputational harm, regulatory penalties, legal liabilities, and operational disruptions. Therefore, managing operational risks is essential for preserving the stability, productivity, and longevity of businesses across all industries. Here are some examples of Operational Risks:

Human Error

Human error is a frequent contributor to operational risk. It can include employee errors such as incorrect data submission, improper transaction processing, or failure to follow established procedures. For instance, if an employee enters the incorrect decimal point in a financial transaction, significant financial losses may result.

System Failures

System failures, such as faulty hardware or software, can disrupt operations and result in operational hazards. For instance, if a banking system encounters a technical error, consumers may be unable to access their accounts or conduct transactions, resulting in service disruptions and potential financial losses.

Cybersecurity Breaches

Cyber threats have become a major operational risk due to the increasing reliance on digital systems and technologies. Cybersecurity breaches, such as hacking, malware attacks, and data intrusions, can compromise sensitive information, disrupt operations, and harm the reputation of an organization. In the 2017 Equifax data breach, for instance, hackers obtained access to the personal information of millions of people, resulting in financial and reputational losses for the company.

Supply Chain Disruptions

Supply chains are crucial to the delivery of products and services by businesses. Any disruption in the supply chain, such as natural disasters, transportation breakdowns, or supplier insolvency, can have a significant effect on operations. For instance, if a manufacturer is highly dependent on a single supplier and that supplier experiences a disruption, the manufacturer may experience production delays or increased costs.

Regulatory and Compliance Issues

There may be operational risks associated with noncompliance with applicable laws, regulations, or industry standards. This includes violations of data protection, safety, financial reporting, and anti-money laundering regulations. Regulatory fines, legal penalties, and reputational injury are potential consequences of non-compliance.

Product or Service Failures

Failures of products or services can also pose operational hazards. A defective product that poses safety risks to consumers, for instance, can result in lawsuits, product recalls, and harm to the manufacturer's reputation. Similarly, a service provider with frequent service interruptions or inadequate customer support may experience customer dissatisfaction and business loss.

It is essential to note that these examples represent only a subset of the operational hazards that organizations may face. Risks associated with operations can vary across industries and even between departments within the same organization. Effective risk management requires the identification, evaluation, and mitigation of operational risks through the implementation of robust internal controls, contingency plans, employee training, and continuous monitoring and improvement processes.

STRATEGIC RISK

Strategic risk is the possibility that events or circumstances will hinder an organization's ability to attain its strategic objectives. It involves inherent risks in the overarching strategic direction, decision-making processes, and competitive positioning of the organization. Strategic risks are frequently of a long-term nature and can have a substantial effect on an organization's reputation, financial performance, and market position.

To better understand strategic risk, let us explore some detailed examples:

Market Disruption

The possibility of market disruptions that render their products or services obsolete or less pertinent is a strategic risk organization face. The rise of digital streaming services, for instance, has disrupted the traditional video rental industry, rendering companies like Blockbuster obsolete. To reduce the risk of losing their competitive advantage, organizations must anticipate and adapt to market shifts.

Technological Change

Rapid technological progress can pose strategic dangers. Companies that do not embrace digital transformation, for instance, run the risk of being left behind by rivals who utilize emergent technologies to improve their products, services, or operational efficiency. Blockbuster's reluctance to adopt online streaming technology contributed to its ultimate demise.

Regulatory Changes

Changes in laws, regulations, or government policies can expose organizations to strategic hazards. For instance, stricter environmental regulations may require businesses to invest in costly improvements or alter their production processes in order to comply, which can have a negative impact on their profitability and competitiveness. Organizations must remain informed and adapt their compliance strategies to evolving regulatory landscapes.

Brand and Reputation Damage

Negative publicity, public perception, or reputational harm can pose strategic risks. For instance, a company involved in a significant product recall due to safety concerns may suffer severe brand reputation damage, resulting in decreased customer trust and market share. These hazards can be mitigated by proactive risk management practices, such as quality control and crisis management plans.

Competitive Disruption

Strategic risks can be posed by the emergence of new competitors or disruptive business models. The rise of ride-sharing platforms such as Uber and Lyft, for instance, has disrupted the taxi industry by providing a more convenient and affordable alternative. Existing transportation companies that failed to adapt to this disruptive innovation ran the risk of losing a substantial portion of the market.

Mergers and Acquisitions

Mergers, acquisitions, and partnerships can present strategic dangers. Integration of diverse organizational cultures, processes, and systems is difficult and may result in operational inefficiency or conflict. Mergers that are poorly executed can result in financial losses, reputational harm, and a decrease in market value.

Economic Factors

Conditions macroeconomic and market fluctuations can pose strategic risks. A sudden economic recession, for instance, can result in decreased consumer expenditure, decreased demand for goods and services, and increased financial instability. Organizations must consider economic factors and create contingency plans to effectively navigate these risks.

To mitigate strategic risks, organizations must conduct exhaustive risk assessments, develop robust risk management strategies, and routinely monitor the external environment for the emergence of new risks.

By proactively identifying and addressing strategic risks, organizations can increase their resilience, preserve their competitive advantage, and achieve long-term success.

COMPLIANCE RISK

Compliance risk is the likelihood that an organization will violate applicable laws, regulations, industry standards, or internal policies and procedures. It results from noncompliance with legal and regulatory requirements, resulting in adverse financial, legal, reputational, and operational outcomes. Compliance risk can impact businesses in a variety of industries and sectors, and its management is essential for sustaining an organization's integrity, ethical practices, and legal compliance.

Compliance risk examples can vary depending on the industry and the applicable regulations. Here are some specific examples:

Financial Industry

Compliance with Anti-Money Laundering (AML) Regulations: Banks and financial institutions must abide by regulations designed to prevent money laundering and terrorist financing. Failure to employ efficient AML procedures may result in severe penalties, reputational harm, and legal repercussions.

Know Your Customer (KYC) Compliance

In order to prevent fraud, identity theft, and illegal activities, financial institutions must verify the identity of their consumers. Inadequate Know Your Customer (KYC) procedures can result in regulatory fines and an increased risk of financial offenses.

Healthcare Industry

Compliance with the Health Insurance Portability and Accountability Act (HIPAA) requires healthcare providers, insurers, and business associates to safeguard patient health information and adhere to HIPAA's privacy and security requirements. Breach of patient confidentiality or failure to implement sufficient safeguards can result in legal liability and reputational damage.

Compliance with Clinical Trials and Research

Organizations conducting clinical trials and research must abide by ethical standards, data protection regulations, and informed consent protocols. Noncompliance can result in legal penalties, the loss of research grants, and reputational harm to the organization.

Information Technology (IT) Industry

Companies handling sensitive customer data, such as confidential information and financial records, must adhere to data protection and privacy regulations, such as the General Data Protection Regulation (GDPR) and the California Consumer Privacy Act (CCPA). Noncompliance may result in hefty fines, legal action, and the loss of consumer confidence.

Compliance with Software Licensing and Intellectual Property: Organizations must assure the correct licensing and use of software applications, as well as respect intellectual property rights. Noncompliance with licensing agreements or copyright laws can result in legal disputes, monetary fines, and reputational harm.

Environmental Industry

Environmental Regulations Compliance: Businesses engaged in activities that influence the environment, such as manufacturing, energy production, or waste disposal, must comply with environmental regulations and acquire the necessary permits. Noncompliance can result in fines, legal action, environmental and public health damage, and legal action.

Employment Practice

Employers must comply with minimum wage, overtime, and employee classification regulations. Infractions can result in lawsuits, back wages, penalties, and reputational harm to the organization. Organizations must adhere to anti-discrimination and equal opportunity laws to ensure that employees and job applicants are treated fairly. Failure to comply may result in lawsuits, monetary penalties, and reputational harm to the organization.

These are only a handful of examples of compliance concerns across industries. Organizations must effectively identify, assess, and manage compliance risks by implementing robust compliance programs, conducting regular audits, providing employee training, and remaining current on applicable regulations and industry best practices. By proactively managing compliance risks, organizations can prevent legal and reputational harm while nurturing a culture of ethical and responsible business practices.

REPUTATIONAL RISK

Reputational risk is the potential for harm to an organization's reputation, brand image, or public perception, resulting in detrimental outcomes such as customer loss, decreased investor confidence, regulatory scrutiny, and decreased market value. It is the perception of stakeholders, including customers, employees, investors, regulators, and the broader public, regarding the actions, behavior, or performance of the organization.

Reputational risk can arise from a variety of situations and sources, and its effects can be substantial and long-lasting. Here are some examples of reputational hazards in detail:

Product Recalls

If a company discovers a defect or safety issue with its products and initiates a recall, it may attract negative media attention, erode consumer confidence, and harm the company's reputation. For instance, the recall of certain automobile models due to defective airbags or tainted food products can tarnish the brand's reputation and result in financial losses.

Ethical Lapses

Reputation can be severely harmed by unethical behavior or dubious business practices. Fraud, bribery, corruption, and environmental violations are some examples. Such misconduct may result in public backlash, legal consequences, and a loss of credibility for the company. Volkswagen's manipulation of emission tests and the resultant damage to its reputation is a notable instance.

Data Breaches and Cybersecurity Incidents

As organizations rely increasingly on digital systems and manage sensitive customer data, data breaches pose a substantial risk to their reputation. Instances in which consumer data is compromised as a result of cyberattacks or inadequate security measures may result in a loss of trust and reputation damage for the organization. Equifax and Facebook's highly publicized data intrusions serve as cautionary tales.

Social Media Backlash

In the interconnected world of today, social media platforms can amplify reputational risks. Negative publicity, viral customer complaints, or public controversies can rapidly spread across social media channels, harming the reputation of an organization. To effectively manage and address issues raised on social media platforms, businesses must be vigilant and responsive.

Executive Misconduct

When senior administrators or other key members of an organization engage in inappropriate behavior, it can have a significant impact on the organization's reputation. Instances of executive fraud, embezzlement, or personal controversies can lead to public scrutiny, erode trust in leadership, and undermine the credibility of the organization.

Poor Customer Service

Consistently providing subpar customer service can be detrimental to a company's reputation. Negative word-of-mouth, online reviews, and social media complaints can spread rapidly, influencing the perception of potential consumers. Poor customer service poses reputational risks for airlines, telecommunications companies, and other service-oriented industries.

Environmental and Social Impact

Reputational risks exist for organizations that are perceived to have a negative impact on the environment or neglect social responsibility. This includes pollution, violations of labor rights, supply chain controversies, and unsustainable practices. In the past, oil disasters, allegations of sweatshops, and companies associated with deforestation caused significant reputational damage.

These examples demonstrate how reputational risk can arise from a variety of events and actions, affecting organizations in various industries. Managing reputational risk requires proactive measures, such as strong corporate governance, ethical practices, and effective crisis communication strategies, as well as a commitment to maintaining positive stakeholder relationships. By addressing reputational risks, organizations can protect their image, preserve trust, and ensure their long-term success.

ENVIRONMENTAL RISK

Environmental risk refers to the potential negative effects of human activities on the environment, ecosystems, and natural resources. A variety of factors, including pollution, resource depletion, climate change, habitat destruction, and the discharge of hazardous substances, contribute to these risks. Environmental hazards can have significant effects on the natural world and human populations, affecting biodiversity, human health, economic stability, and the quality of life. Here are some detailed examples of environmental risks:

Air Pollution

The emission of pollutants into the atmosphere from a variety of sources, including industrial emissions, vehicle exhaust, and the combustion of fossil fuels, can pose environmental hazards. Air pollution can contribute to respiratory diseases, smog formation, and the depletion of the ozone layer, causing long-term environmental damage and endangering human and animal health.

Water Contamination

The contamination of water bodies, such as rivers, lakes, and groundwater, with contaminants such as chemicals, heavy metals, and untreated sewage, can have severe environmental repercussions. It can disrupt aquatic ecosystems, impair marine life, contaminate sources of drinking water, and contribute to the spread of waterborne diseases.

Soil Degradation

Soil degradation can be caused by unsustainable agricultural practices, deforestation, and industrial activities. Soil erosion, nutrient depletion, and contamination can lead to decreased crop yield, biodiversity loss, and increased susceptibility to floods and droughts.

Climate Change

Increased greenhouse gas emissions, predominantly as a result of human activities, have contributed to global warming. Significant environmental threats are posed by rising global temperatures, altered precipitation patterns, and extreme weather events. These threats include a rise in sea level, an increase in the frequency and intensity of hurricanes, droughts, heat waves, and disruptions to ecosystems and biodiversity.

Habitat Destruction

The transformation of natural habitats such as forests and wetlands into urban areas, agriculture, and infrastructure initiatives results in habitat destruction. This habitat loss threatens biodiversity and disrupts ecosystems, threatening the survival of plant and animal species and diminishing the overall resilience of ecosystems.

Hazardous Waste Disposal

Environmental risks are posed by the improper management, storage, and disposal of hazardous waste from industries, healthcare facilities, and households. Radioactive substances, heavy metals, and toxic compounds can contaminate soil, water, and air, endangering human health, wildlife, and ecosystems.

Natural Resource Depletion

The extraction and consumption of natural resources, such as fossil fuels, minerals, and water, which are not sustainable, contribute to environmental hazards. Overexploitation can result in resource depletion, ecosystem degradation, and resource-related conflict.

Biodiversity Loss

Loss of biodiversity is caused by human activities such as habitat devastation, pollution, invasive species, and climate change. This extinction of plant and animal species endangers ecosystem stability, disrupts ecological processes, and diminishes ecosystems' resistance to environmental changes.

Through effective environmental policies, regulations, sustainable practices, and conservation efforts, it is essential to comprehend and manage these environmental hazards. We can preserve and defend our environment for future generations by identifying and addressing these risks.

TECHNOLOGICAL RISK

Technological risk refers to the possible hazards and uncertainties connected with the use of technology in different parts of our life, such as company operations, information systems, infrastructure, and the entire digital landscape. These hazards result from variables such as technology failures, cybersecurity breaches, data breaches, system malfunctions, and the rapid speed of technological innovation. Financial losses, reputational damage, legal challenges, and disruptions to key services are all possible outcomes of technological hazards.

Here are some specific examples of technical risks:

Cybersecurity Breaches

With the increased reliance on technology, cybersecurity breaches have become a big worry. These breaches can result in unauthorized access to sensitive information, data theft, financial fraud, and the disruption of essential systems. Examples include hacking incidents, malware assaults, ransomware attacks, and phishing scams that exploit vulnerabilities in software, networks, or human behavior.

Data Breach and Privacy Concerns

Organizations collect and retain massive volumes of sensitive data, such as personal information, financial records, and intellectual property. Data breaches occur when this information is compromised, whether through hacking, insider threats, or unintentional exposures. Data breaches not only cause financial losses, but they can also jeopardize people's privacy, undermine customer trust, and result in legal and regulatory ramifications.

System Failures and Downtime

Failures and downtime can occur in technological systems, including hardware, software, and networks, due to a variety of circumstances such as power outages, hardware malfunctions, software flaws, or programming errors. These failures can disrupt business operations, result in financial losses, and have a negative influence on consumer satisfaction. Examples include website crashes, network outages, and failures in essential infrastructure systems such as transportation or healthcare.

Emerging Technology Risks

As new technologies arise, they bring with them both opportunities and threats. The adoption of artificial intelligence (AI) and machine learning, for example, brings dangers such as biased decision-making algorithms, a lack of transparency, and potential job displacements. Similarly, the growth of Internet of Things (IoT) devices raises worries about data security, privacy, and the possibility of unwanted access or control of linked equipment.

Technological Disruptions and Dependency

Technological breakthroughs have the potential to disrupt conventional industries and business strategies. Organizations that do not adapt to technological developments risk becoming obsolete. Furthermore, there is a risk of over-reliance on technology, with a single point of failure having cascading implications. Severe disruption in cloud computing services, for example, can affect several firms that rely heavily on them.

Supply Chain and Infrastructure Vulnerabilities

Technological hazards can affect whole supply chains and essential infrastructure, rather than just individual firms. A cyber assault on a logistics company, for example, can interrupt the movement of goods and harm several organizations. Similarly, flaws in vital infrastructure systems, such as electricity grids or transportation networks, can cause widespread disruptions with serious economic and societal effects. It is critical for enterprises and people to identify and handle technological hazards proactively. This includes establishing effective cybersecurity safeguards, conducting regular risk assessments, maintaining up-to-date on emerging threats and vulnerabilities, and developing contingency plans to mitigate the possible implications of technology hazards.

It is essential to note that the likelihood and severity of risk can vary. Some hazards are more likely and have greater potential consequences, whereas others may be less likely or have fewer repercussions. Effective risk management entails evaluating and prioritizing risks based on their likelihood and impact, and implementing the most suitable strategies to mitigate or manage them.

By comprehending and proactively managing risks, individuals and organizations can make informed decisions, reduce vulnerabilities, seize opportunities, and improve their overall resilience.

In the field of risk management, it is critical to recognize that not all risks are necessarily bad or destructive to a company. While risks are frequently connected with potential harm, they can also bring chances for growth, innovation, and competitive advantage. Understanding the concept of risk appetite and creating a healthy risk culture are critical components in efficiently navigating the risk environment and maximizing the potential benefits.

Risk appetite refers to the level of risk that an organization is ready to accept or tolerate in order to achieve its goals. It reflects the organization's strategic goals, values, and the level of risk it is willing to accept to attain its intended outcomes. Risk appetite guides decision-makers by setting risk-taking boundaries and thresholds, guaranteeing a balanced approach that avoids extreme risk aversion or reckless behavior.

Organizations that have a clear and well-defined risk appetite can make informed judgments about prospective possibilities and dangers. Organizations can align their risk management activities with their strategic objectives and avoid unnecessary exposure or missed opportunities by developing an acceptable risk appetite. It also allows for effective communication and awareness of risk tolerance within the organization, helping workers to make risk-informed decisions within the scope of their jobs and responsibilities.

Risk culture refers to an organization's risk-related attitudes, values, beliefs, and practices. It embodies the collective risk-management philosophy and strategy that pervades the whole firm, from top-level executives to front-line personnel. A strong risk culture produces an atmosphere in which risk is viewed as an inherent aspect of decision-making and individuals are empowered to detect, assess, and manage risks effectively.

A positive risk culture promotes open communication, transparency, and accountability when it comes to risks. It fosters a proactive mindset in which risks are addressed, evaluated, and integrated into the organization's strategic planning processes. A strong risk culture also promotes a continual learning and improvement mindset, in which lessons from previous events are shared and implemented to improve future risk management processes.

Notably, risk culture should relate to the organization's principles and integrated into its entire corporate culture. It should be backed by suitable policies, processes, and governance structures that promote risk awareness and prudent risk-taking at all levels of the company.

THE SYNERGY OF RISK APPETITE AND RISK CULTURE

Both risk appetite and risk culture are interrelated and mutually reinforcing. The values, attitudes, and behaviors of individuals inside an organization determine the organization's overall risk tolerance and appetite. In contrast, an organization's risk appetite helps shape its risk culture by providing a framework and rules for risk management procedures and decision-making processes.

Organizations may efficiently capitalize on opportunities while managing potential risks when their risk appetite and risk culture are matched and well-integrated. They foster a climate in which risk is viewed as a benefit rather than a burden to doing business. This proactive approach enables firms to recognize new risks, react to changing situations, and make educated decisions to enhance value generation while limiting potential negative repercussions.

Finally, knowing the ideas of risk appetite and risk culture, as well as recognizing that not all risks are bad, are critical for effective risk management. Organizations may grab opportunities, promote innovation, and succeed in an uncertain and ever-changing business environment by having a defined risk appetite and building a positive risk culture.

WHAT IS RISK MANAGEMENT?

Risk management is the ongoing process of identifying, assessing, prioritizing, and addressing risks to minimize their potential negative impact and maximize opportunities. It is a proactive and strategic approach to dealing with uncertainties, aimed at reducing the likelihood of adverse events and minimizing the potential consequences if they do occur. Risk management involves not only addressing known risks but also anticipating and preparing for potential future risks. It requires a combination of knowledge, skills, methodologies, and tools to effectively navigate the complex landscape of risks and make informed decisions.

The field of risk assessment and risk management is multidisciplinary, drawing from various disciplines such as finance, economics, engineering, psychology, and environmental sciences. It encompasses a wide range of activities, including risk identification, risk analysis, risk evaluation, risk treatment, risk communication, and risk monitoring. Depending on the nature of the risks and the context in which they occur, different techniques and approaches may be employed, such as qualitative assessments, quantitative modeling, scenario analysis, and decision trees.

Effective risk management and risk assessment have numerous benefits. They help organizations identify potential threats and opportunities, enhance decision-making processes, allocate resources effectively, improve project planning, and enhance overall performance and resilience. Risk management also enables organizations to comply with regulatory requirements, maintain stakeholder confidence, and adapt to changing business environments.

As risk management is a continuous process, it requires a proactive and systematic approach. It involves establishing a risk management framework, defining risk appetite and tolerance levels, implementing risk management strategies, regularly monitoring and reviewing risks, and adjusting mitigation plans as necessary. It also requires effective communication and collaboration among stakeholders to ensure a shared understanding of risks and facilitate informed decision-making.

Risk assessment and risk management are essential disciplines that enable individuals and organizations to navigate uncertainties and make informed decisions in a dynamic world. By identifying, analyzing, and mitigating risks, organizations can protect their assets, enhance their performance, and seize opportunities for growth and innovation. The study and practice of risk assessment and risk management provide valuable skills and knowledge that can be applied across industries and sectors, making it an indispensable field in today's rapidly evolving landscape.

WHY DO WE NEED RISK MANAGEMENT?

Risk management is essential for businesses and individuals for a variety of reasons:

PROTECTION AGAINST UNCERTAINTY

In a world of perpetual change and unpredictability, individuals, businesses, and organizations must defend themselves from uncertainty. The lack of understanding or predictability about future events, consequences, or conditions is referred to as uncertainty. Economic fluctuations, technology improvements, natural calamities, regulatory changes, and geopolitical movements can all cause it. Individuals and entities use a variety of methods and preventive measures to alleviate the negative impact of uncertainty. In this note, we will look at many examples of uncertainty protection in various circumstances.

Personal Financial Protection

- Emergency Reserve: Individuals can establish an emergency fund by putting a portion of their salary aside to cover unforeseen expenses such as medical crises, auto repairs, or temporary job loss. This acts as a safety net and decreases the financial load during times of uncertainty.

- Insurance: Health insurance, life insurance, property insurance, and disability insurance all provide protection against unanticipated calamities. They provide financial protection and help limit potential financial losses caused by accidents, diseases, natural disasters, or other bad events.

- Diversification of Investments: Individuals can limit the risk of severe losses from a single investment by diversifying their investment portfolio among several asset classes. This method helps to protect against financial market instability.

Business Risk Management

- Risk Evaluation: Businesses perform risk assessments in order to detect potential threats and vulnerabilities that may impact their operations. Businesses can build ways to limit or transfer risks by understanding them, ensuring continuity and stability in uncertain environments.

- Contingency Planning: Businesses develop contingency plans in order to deal with anticipated disruptions or disasters. These plans detail alternative courses of action, resource allocation techniques, and communication procedures to ensure that the company can respond to unforeseen occurrences efficiently.

- Supply Chain Resilience: Companies frequently diversify their supply chains by collaborating with multiple vendors or establishing backup vendors. This technique safeguards against supply chain disruptions such as natural catastrophes, political instability, or economic crises.

Government Measures

- Fiscal Policy: Governments may pursue expansionary fiscal policies, such as increased government spending and tax cuts, during economic downturns to encourage economic growth and relieve uncertainty. These policies are intended to restore consumer and corporate confidence, stabilize financial markets, and foster an atmosphere conducive to economic recovery.

- Regulatory Frameworks: Governments create regulations and frameworks to keep consumers, investors, and businesses safe from uncertainty. These rules may include, among other things, consumer protection legislation, financial restrictions, environmental standards, and labor laws. Governments help to reduce uncertainty for businesses and individuals by establishing a stable and predictable regulatory framework.

Technological Change

- Research and development: Embracing technology breakthroughs and investing in R&D operations can assist firms in staying ahead of the curve and adapting to changing market conditions. Businesses can insulate themselves from uncertainty caused by disruptive technologies or changing customer preferences by constantly inventing and researching new technologies.

- Cybersecurity: The risk of cyber threats and data breaches grows as technology becomes more interwoven into corporate operations. Implementing strong cybersecurity measures protects businesses and individuals from the uncertainty associated with future cyber-attacks, while also securing sensitive data and ensuring operational continuity.

These examples demonstrate how uncertainty protection is important in many facets of life, including personal money, corporate operations, and government regulations. Individuals and organizations can navigate uncertainty more successfully and mitigate its potential negative implications by implementing proactive solutions. Embracing risk management tactics, investing in insurance, diversifying investments, and capitalizing on technological breakthroughs are all valuable ways to mitigate uncertainty and boost resilience in an ever-changing world.

DECISION MAKING

Making decisions is an essential part of our everyday life, both individually and professionally. Every day, we are presented with a plethora of options that need us to weigh various alternatives, analyze prospective outcomes, and finally decide. A methodical approach to decision-making that incorporates available information evaluates risks and benefits, and corresponds with our aims and beliefs is required for effective decision-making. In this note, we will look at the decision-making process and present specific examples to demonstrate various decision-making strategies and scenarios.

Rational Decision-Making

Rational decision-making is a methodical process that entails obtaining relevant information, recognizing alternatives, weighing their advantages and disadvantages, and picking the optimal option. This method is frequently utilized in business and organizational contexts. As an example: Consider yourself a project manager in charge of picking a software development vendor for a key project. You would conduct research, gather proposals from various vendors, evaluate their capabilities, consider factors such as cost, quality, and expertise, and finally select the vendor that best aligns with the project requirements and organizational goals.

Making Intuitive Decisions

Without a rigorous study, intuitive decision-making depends on instinct, gut feelings, and past experiences to make choices. This method is useful when time is limited or the decision is based on subjective criteria. As an example: When negotiating a transaction with a client, as an experienced salesperson, you may rely on your intuition. You may make quick decisions regarding pricing, product positioning, and concessions based on your gut feelings and a sense of what has worked in comparable situations, drawing on your expertise and knowledge of the market.

Making Decisions Together

Collaborative decision-making entails involving numerous stakeholders and soliciting their thoughts and opinions in order to reach an agreement. This method is useful when multiple perspectives and skills are necessary to make an informed conclusion. Consider the following scenario: Team members may engage in collaborative decision-making in a team-based project by conducting regular meetings, brainstorming ideas, discussing various choices, and collectively agreeing on the best course of action. Each team member provides their own unique perspective, and they work together to reach a consensus that benefits the entire team.

Making Ethical Decisions

Ethical decision-making entails considering moral principles, values, and ethical standards while making decisions. This method ensures that judgments are ethical and have a good influence on individuals and society. Here is an illustration: The management team of a corporation is faced with the decision to lay off many people in order to save money. Ethical decision-making would include considering the influence on employees, their families, and the larger community. Decision-makers would assess the financial necessity against the ethical responsibility to treat employees fairly, to provide support, and explore options to mitigate the negative impact.

Making Risk-Based Decisions

Assessing the risks and uncertainties associated with several options and selecting the one with the best risk-reward tradeoff is what risk-based decision-making entails. This method is frequently employed in financial and project management contexts. Consider the following scenario: An investor is weighing the pros and cons of two investment opportunities: one with possibly larger returns but higher risks, and one with lower profits but reduced dangers. To make an informed decision that balances risk and return based on their risk appetite and investment objectives, the investor would undertake a risk assessment, examining factors such as market volatility, industry trends, and regulatory changes.

Making good decisions is an important ability to have in both personal and professional situations. Individuals and organizations can negotiate difficult situations, manage risks, and achieve their goals by understanding and employing diverse decision-making approaches such as logical, intuitive, collaborative, ethical, and risk-based decision-making. Consider the examples offered to get insight into the practical implementation of these decision-making techniques.

INCREASING RESILIENCE

In the context of risk management, resilience refers to an individual's, organization's, or community's ability to endure and recover from unfavorable events or disruptions. It entails developing strong systems, procedures, and strategies that allow entities to adapt, absorb shocks, and continue to operate effectively in the face of adversity. In today's dynamic and uncertain climate, improving resilience has become a vital objective for long-term success and sustainability. This essay delves into the notion of resilience and offers specific examples of how it might be improved in various sectors.

Resilience in Business

- Diversification: A business that is overly reliant on a single product or market is vulnerable to change. Diversifying product offerings or expanding into new areas can help to lessen reliance on a single source of revenue.

- Logistics Management: Building supply chain resilience entails recognizing and reducing risks, developing backup sources, and cultivating strong relationships with critical partners. Following the Fukushima nuclear tragedy, for example, many corporations updated their supply chain strategies to lessen their reliance on Japanese suppliers.

- Planning for Business Continuity: Implementing solid business continuity planning assists firms in keeping operations running during and after disruptions. Backup systems, other work sites, and extensive crisis management protocols are examples of such measures.

Cybersecurity

- Planning an Incident Response: Creating an efficient incident response plan allows firms to recognize, respond to, and recover rapidly from cyber threats. Defining roles and duties, performing frequent drills, and investing in sophisticated threat detection and response capabilities are all part of the process.

- Data security and backup: Strong data protection techniques, such as encryption and access controls, aid in the protection of essential information. Data recovery is ensured through regular backups and off-site storage of data in the case of a breach or system failure.

- Employee Education and Training: To increase resilience to cyber attacks, staff must be educated on best practices such as avoiding phishing emails, using strong passwords, and exercising good online hygiene. Regular training programs can help firms foster a security-conscious culture.

Resilience of the Community

- Disaster Planning: Investing in infrastructure, early warning systems, and emergency response skills can help communities become more resilient. To lessen the impact of disasters, coastal areas prone to storms might construct seawalls, prepare evacuation strategies, and hold regular drills.

- Collaboration and social cohesion: Resilience is enhanced by strong social networks and community involvement. Communities that encourage linkages and collaborations between individuals, local businesses, and government agencies are better prepared to respond to and recover from disasters.

- Economic Diversification: Communities that rely too heavily on a single industry suffer major hazards. Encouragement of economic diversification and support for different sector growth can improve resilience by lowering vulnerability to economic downturns.

Individual Resilience

- Mindset for Adaptation: Developing a resilient attitude entails accepting change, remaining optimistic, and building flexibility and adaptation in the face of adversity. This perspective enables people to recover from losses and see chances in adversity.

- Personal Happiness: Taking care of one's physical and mental health helps one's resilience. Regular exercise, enough rest, mindfulness, and seeking assistance from friends and family can all help people manage stress and retain resilience.

- Lifelong Education: Continuous learning and the acquisition of new abilities increase human resilience by allowing people to adapt to changing circumstances and seize opportunities. Personal resilience is enhanced through embracing new technologies, remaining current on industry trends, and seeking professional growth.

These examples demonstrate how resilience can be improved across multiple areas. Individuals, organizations, and communities can handle uncertainty, recover from setbacks, and prosper in a fast-changing world by applying resilience methods and measures. Building resilience is a continuous process that necessitates a proactive attitude, forward-thinking solutions, and a willingness to learn and adapt.

COMPLIANCE AND MANAGEMENT

Compliance and management are critical components of good organizational governance. The observance of laws, regulations, policies, and industry standards that regulate an organization's operations is referred to as compliance. It guarantees that organizations perform ethically and responsibly, reducing the dangers of legal infractions, reputational loss, and financial penalties. Compliance management entails the development, implementation, and monitoring of processes and systems to ensure consistent compliance. In this section, we will discuss the significance of compliance and management, as well as provide specific instances of their practical implementations. Here are some examples:

Regulatory Adherence

Regulatory compliance is critical in heavily regulated areas such as banking, healthcare, and energy. As an example:

- To combat fraud, money laundering, and terrorist funding, banks and financial institutions must follow regulations such as the Basel III framework, anti-money laundering (AML) statutes, and Know Your Customer (KYC) standards.
- To safeguard patient information and defend their privacy rights, firms in the healthcare industry must follow data privacy rules

such as the Health Insurance Portability and Accountability Act (HIPAA) in the United States.

- To reduce their environmental impact and maintain sustainable practices, energy businesses must follow environmental rules such as emissions limits and waste management requirements.

Compliance with Occupational Health and Safety (OHS)

- OHS laws must be followed in order to maintain a safe and healthy working environment. Organizations must create safety measures, conduct frequent inspections, and provide enough personnel training. Here are several examples:

- To reduce accidents and injuries on building sites, construction companies must follow safety rules. This involves using personal protective equipment (PPE), holding frequent safety meetings, and putting in place fall prevention measures.

- To safeguard workers from potential risks linked with heavy machinery, electrical hazards, and poisonous substances, manufacturing facilities must follow machinery safety standards, electrical safety rules, and hazardous material handling requirements.

Data Security and Privacy Regulations

As information becomes more digital, enterprises must comply with data protection and privacy rules to secure personal and sensitive data. Here are several examples:

- In the European Union, the General Data Protection Regulation (GDPR) requires enterprises to get consent for data gathering, keep data securely, and notify individuals in the event of a data breach.

- The California Consumer Privacy Act (CCPA), which provides customers control over their personal information and requires transparent data management procedures, requires social media platforms and technology corporations to comply with privacy requirements.

Compliance with Ethical Standards

- Ethical compliance entails following ethical standards as well as industry codes of behavior. Organizations develop ethical standards to encourage fairness, integrity, and appropriate business operations. Here are several examples:

- Companies may have anti-bribery and corruption rules that require staff to refrain from proposing or receiving bribes in order to secure business deals.

- Companies in the pharmaceutical sector must follow ethical norms governing clinical studies, patient consent, and drug pricing to protect patient safety and public trust.

Compliance and management are critical in ensuring that firms follow legal and ethical guidelines. Organizations can mitigate risks, defend their brand, and demonstrate their commitment to responsible business practices by developing strong compliance frameworks. The examples offered demonstrate the various areas in which compliance and management are significant, but it is important to recognize that compliance standards may differ among industries, geographies, and organizational contexts. Organizations may develop an integrity culture, reduce risks, and improve overall performance by prioritizing compliance and establishing effective management systems.

COST SAVINGS AND RESOURCE MANAGEMENT

Saving money and managing resources are critical components of efficient financial management and organizational sustainability. Businesses can improve their profitability, operational efficiency, and long-term growth through maximizing resource allocation and decreasing expenses. In this note, we will discuss the significance of cost savings and resource management, as well as provide extensive examples to demonstrate their value in diverse circumstances.

Importance of Cost Savings

Cost savings are critical to preserving a competitive advantage and maximizing profitability. Organizations can spend resources more efficiently and earn greater margins by finding areas where expenses can be lowered without sacrificing quality or performance. Here are a few examples of cost-cutting measures:

Process Improvements

Organizations may eliminate unnecessary procedures, decrease waste, and save both time and money by assessing and optimizing business processes. Implementing lean manufacturing concepts, for example, can help reduce production costs and increase productivity.

Supplier Contract Negotiation

Negotiating favorable contracts with suppliers can result in significant cost savings. To lower procurement costs, organizations can seek better pricing, volume discounts, or preferential payment terms. By raising order numbers, a retailer, for example, might negotiate cheaper rates with wholesalers or suppliers.

Energy Efficiency Initiatives

Putting in place energy-saving practices and technologies can result in significant cost reductions over time. Organizations should invest in energy-efficient technology, encourage staff conservation, and investigate renewable energy possibilities. For example, switching to LED lights or installing solar panels can help you save money on electricity.

Digital Transformation

Adopting digital technologies can help to streamline operations, reduce paper use, and save costs. Organizations, for example, can save money on storage, printing, and document handling by implementing cloud computing solutions, automated workflows, and electronic document management systems.

Resource Management

Optimizing the allocation and exploitation of various resources within an organization is what effective resource management entails. This encompasses human capital, materials, equipment, and time, in addition to financial resources.

Here are some strategies for resource management:

Workforce Optimization

It is critical for efficient resource management to match workforce numbers to task needs. Organizations can utilize workforce planning tools and strategies to estimate demand, properly schedule staff, and save labor expenditures. Implementing flexible work arrangements or cross-training staff, for example, can boost productivity while lowering overtime costs.

Inventory Management

It is critical to manage inventory levels in order to avoid excess inventory costs and stockouts. Inventory management systems can be used by businesses to oversee stock levels, monitor demand patterns, and adopt just-in-time inventory techniques. Businesses can minimize carrying costs and improve cash flow by optimizing inventory levels.

Outsourcing and Collaborations

Outsourcing non-core functions or partnering with strategic partners can save money and provide access to specialized skills. Organizations can use outsourcing to cut expenses, improve operational efficiencies, and focus on core capabilities. A software development company, for example, may outsource customer support to a specialist call center.

Time Management

Effective time management is essential for increasing production and reducing resource waste. To improve employee performance, organizations might use time-tracking systems, prioritize activities, and set firm deadlines. Businesses can save money by eliminating time-wasting tasks and strengthening time management abilities.

For firms to attain financial stability and long-term performance, cost savings and resource management are critical. Businesses can achieve significant cost savings and maximize resource efficiency by implementing strategies such as streamlining processes, negotiating contracts, promoting energy efficiency, embracing digital transformation, optimizing workforce, managing inventory, outsourcing, and practicing effective time management. Organizations must constantly monitor and review their cost-cutting initiatives and resource allocation methods in order to react to changing market conditions and maintain a competitive advantage.

STAKEHOLDER CONFIDENCE

Stakeholder trust is essential to the success of any company or endeavor. It relates to stakeholders' trust, contentment, and belief in the organization's ability to keep promises, achieve results, and act in their best interests. Building and sustaining stakeholder trust is critical for developing strong connections, gaining support, and attaining long-term sustainability.

Other persons and groups are examples of stakeholders. Each stakeholder group may have different expectations and worries; thus, it is critical for companies to recognize and satisfy their distinct needs in order to create trust.

Here are a few significant characteristics that contribute to stakeholder trust, along with instances of their importance:

Transparency and Communication

Building stakeholder trust requires open and transparent communication. Transparency is demonstrated by organizations that provide regular updates, share pertinent information, and engage in two-way communication. A corporation that releases quarterly reports and holds town hall meetings to address employee problems, for example, promotes trust and confidence among its employees.

Accountability and Ethical Behavior

Gaining stakeholder trust requires demonstrating responsibility and ethical behavior. Organizations that follow ethical norms, accept responsibility for their activities, and handle any misconduct swiftly foster confidence. For example, a financial institution that responds quickly to client concerns and takes steps to avoid fraud increases trust in its services.

Consistent delivery of promises

Delivering pledges and commitments on a consistent basis is critical for stakeholder trust. Organizations that consistently meet or exceed customer expectations for quality, service, and delivery develop a reputation for dependability. For example, an e-commerce platform that consistently delivers things on time and has a simple return process earns its consumers' trust.

Stakeholder Engagement

Engaging stakeholders in decision-making processes and soliciting their feedback indicates respect and appreciation for their perspectives. Organizations that actively engage stakeholders in the development of strategies or policies foster a sense of ownership and confidence. A local administration, for example, hosting public forums to obtain input on urban planning initiatives demonstrates a commitment to involving the community and creating trust.

Risk Management and Crisis Management

Effective risk management and crisis response are critical for sustaining stakeholder trust during difficult times. Organizations that proactively identify and manage risks, as well as respond quickly and transparently during crises, inspire trust. A pharmaceutical business, for example, that efficiently controls and discusses possible product safety risks develops trust in its commitment to consumer health.

Social Responsibility

Stakeholder trust is increased by demonstrating social responsibility and sustainable practices. Stakeholders trust and support organizations that value environmental sustainability, social impact, and ethical sourcing. For example, a fashion company that uses fair trade procedures and encourages environmentally friendly production processes instills trust in its dedication to ethical business practices.

Open communication, ethical practices, accountability, consistent delivery, stakeholder involvement, effective risk management, and social responsibility are the foundations of stakeholder confidence. Organizations that prioritize these characteristics and actively work to address stakeholder concerns and expectations will be better positioned to win and keep their stakeholders' trust and confidence, resulting in long-term success and sustainability.

POSSIBILITIES FOR INNOVATION AND DEVELOPMENT

Organizations continuously seek possibilities for innovation and development in today's dynamic and competitive world in order to stay relevant, build a competitive advantage, and drive growth. Adopting an innovative mindset and actively pursuing development initiatives can result in dramatic improvements, increased efficiencies, and increased value generation. In this note, we will look at the opportunities for innovation and development, as well as provide specific examples to demonstrate their value.

Technological Advancements

Technology is a major driver of innovation and growth. Artificial intelligence (AI), robotics, blockchain, and the Internet of Things (IoT) advancements give enormous opportunities for enterprises to revolutionize their operations, improve goods and services, and streamline processes. For example, by combining AI and machine learning algorithms, businesses may analyze enormous amounts of data and acquire important insights for tailored customer experiences, predictive maintenance, and better decision- making. Robotic process automation (RPA) is used by a manufacturing organization to automate repetitive processes on the assembly line, minimizing errors, increasing efficiency, and freeing personnel to focus on higher-value activities.

New Product or Service Offerings

Creating innovative products or services can help you enter new markets, attract clients, and increase your revenue. Organizations can create unique solutions that fulfill unmet needs or provide superior alternatives to existing services by recognizing client demands, harnessing market trends, and investing in research and development (R&D). This strategy enables businesses to differentiate themselves and grab new market segments. For example: A subscription-based personalized styling service is introduced by an e- commerce platform, in which users receive handpicked fashion goods tailored to their preferences and body type. This service offers convenience, personalized recommendations, and a more enjoyable purchasing experience.

Process Optimization and Automation

Streamlining and automating corporate operations can lead to considerable benefits in efficiency, cost savings, and increased customer satisfaction. Organizations may automate manual activities, eliminate redundancies, and enhance overall efficiency by examining existing workflows, identifying bottlenecks, and employing technology. For example: A bank installs a digital document management system, replacing paper-based operations with automated workflows. This modification improves document processing time, eliminates errors, and allows for seamless team collaboration.

Collaborative Partnerships and Alliances

Collaboration with outside partners, such as colleagues in the industry, startups, research institutes, or even customers, can drive innovation and development. Organizations can speed up the pace of innovation, get access to new technologies or markets, and share risks and gains by pooling resources, skills, and viewpoints. For example: To create autonomous driving capabilities for their vehicles, an automotive manufacturer collaborates with a technology company. This relationship combines the automotive experience of the manufacturer with the advanced sensors and algorithms of the technology business, resulting in the development of unique self-driving features.

Sustainable and Environmental Initiatives

Organizations have the chance to innovate and develop solutions to solve sustainability and environmental concerns as they gain popularity. Organizations can demonstrate social responsibility while meeting the growing market need for sustainable solutions by implementing environmentally friendly processes, manufacturing eco-friendly products, and embracing renewable energy sources. For example: A food packaging company uses biodegradable and compostable materials to replace standard plastic packaging, decreasing environmental impact and matching consumer desires for sustainable packaging solutions.

Customer Experience Enhancements

Efforts in innovation and development can be directed at bettering the whole customer experience. Organizations may discover pain spots and develop new solutions that give outstanding experiences, ease, and personalization by employing technology, obtaining customer input, and monitoring user behavior. For example: A retail store installs a Smartphone app that enables consumers to scan things, receive personalized recommendations, and make payments in real-time. This technologically driven strategy improves convenience, expedites the checkout process, and gives a more personalized shopping experience.

The opportunities for innovation and development are numerous and diverse. To promote growth and stay ahead of the market, organizations might investigate technical advancements, develop new product or service offerings, optimize processes, form collaborative alliances, embrace sustainability, and improve customer experiences. Organizations may unlock their potential, adapt to shifting needs, and survive in an ever-changing business landscape by embracing an innovative culture.

CHAPTER 2

Risk Identification and Assessment

IDENTIFICATION of risks is the essential first stage in risk management. It involves meticulously identifying and documenting potential risks that could have an impact on the accomplishment of organizational objectives or project outcomes. By proactively identifying risks, organizations can develop strategies to mitigate or exploit them, thereby improving their capacity to respond effectively to unanticipated events.

During the risk identification phase, it is crucial to involve stakeholders from a variety of organizational levels in order to collect diverse perspectives and ensure comprehensive coverage of potential risks. This inclusive approach facilitates a more in-depth comprehension of the organization's operations, processes, and external environment, allowing for a more comprehensive risk assessment.

There are numerous techniques and methods available for identifying hazards. Here are some prevalent approaches:

Brainstorming

This method entails assembling a group of individuals with diverse expertise and knowledge in order to generate a list of potential dangers. The participants communicate their ideas freely, fostering creative thought and revealing risks that may not have been initially apparent.

Documentation Evaluation

By evaluating organizational documents such as policies, procedures, project plans, and historical data, valuable insights into past incidents, issues, or obstacles can be gained. This analysis aids in the identification of recurrent risks or those associated with activities or processes.

Surveys and Interviews

Interviewing or surveying key stakeholders can provide valuable insight into their experiences, concerns, and risk perceptions. This method assists in identifying risks that may not be immediately apparent and provides a qualitative comprehension of the impact and probability of identified risks.

Checklists

Using predefined protocols or risk registers can facilitate the systematic identification of risks based on industry standards, regulations, or past experiences. Checklists serve as a guide to guarantee that common hazards are not missed during the identification process.

SWOT Analysis

SWOT Analysis is a powerful strategic planning tool used to evaluate the strengths, weaknesses, opportunities, and threats of an individual, organization, or project. By conducting a SWOT Analysis, one can gain valuable insights into the internal and external factors that can influence their objectives and decision-making processes. This note will provide a detailed explanation of each component of the SWOT Analysis, along with illustrative examples.

Strengths

Strengths refer to the internal positive attributes or capabilities that give an individual, organization, or project a competitive advantage. These are factors that contribute to success and differentiation. Examples of strengths may include:

- Strong brand reputation and recognition.
- Skilled and experienced workforce.
- High-quality products or services.
- Robust financial position.
- Efficient supply chain management.
- Effective internal communication and teamwork.

Weaknesses

Weaknesses are internal factors that hinder an individual, organization, or project from achieving optimal performance or competitive advantage. Identifying weaknesses allows for targeted improvement efforts. Examples of weaknesses may include:

- The limited market presence or brand awareness.
- Lack of technological infrastructure.
- Inadequate financial resources.
- Inefficient operational processes.
- Skill gaps or insufficient training.
- Poor customer service.

Opportunities

Opportunities are external factors that present favorable circumstances for growth, expansion, or improvement. Identifying opportunities enables individuals or organizations to capitalize on emerging trends or market conditions. Examples of opportunities may include:

- New market segments or untapped customer demographics.
- Technological advancements can improve efficiency.
- Changes in government regulations or policies.
- Collaborative partnerships or strategic alliances.
- Growing demand for a particular product or service.
- Economic or market trends that align with existing capabilities.

Threats

Threats are external factors that pose challenges or risks to an individual, organization, or project's success. Identifying threats allows for proactive planning and risk mitigation strategies. Examples of threats may include:

- Intense competition within the industry.
- Economic downturns or market volatility.
- Rapid technological advancements render current offerings obsolete.
- Changing consumer preferences or buying behavior.
- Legal or regulatory challenges.
- Supplier or vendor reliability issues.

It is important to note that strengths and weaknesses are internal to the individual or organization, while opportunities and threats are external factors in the broader environment. The goal of conducting a SWOT Analysis is to leverage strengths, address weaknesses, capitalize on opportunities, and mitigate threats to develop effective strategies and make informed decisions.

By considering the combination of internal strengths and weaknesses with external opportunities and threats, individuals and organizations can develop actionable plans that align with their objectives and maximize their chances of success.

SWOT Analysis provides a comprehensive framework for assessing the current state and future prospects of an individual, organization, or project. It helps identify key areas for improvement, potential growth avenues, and risks to be managed. Through a thoughtful and thorough SWOT Analysis, individuals and organizations can gain valuable insights that inform their strategic decision-making processes.

Scenario Analysis

Processes to explore various potential future outcomes and their associated risks and opportunities. It involves the creation of multiple plausible scenarios or narratives to evaluate the potential impact of different factors and events on a given situation or project. By considering a range of scenarios, organizations can enhance their preparedness, identify potential vulnerabilities, and develop effective strategies to navigate uncertain environments.

Here are some examples of Scenario Analysis:

- *Financial Sector*

  Imagine a scenario where a global recession occurs due to a major financial crisis. In this scenario, interest rates rise, stock markets crash, and credit becomes tight. Financial institutions face increased default risks, liquidity challenges, and regulatory pressures. By conducting scenario analysis, banks and investment firms can assess their vulnerability to such a situation and develop contingency plans to ensure their financial stability, such as diversifying their investment portfolios, stress-testing their balance sheets, and strengthening risk management practices.

- *Energy Industry*

  Consider a scenario where there is a significant disruption in the global oil supply due to political tensions or natural disasters.

This scenario leads to a sudden increase in oil prices, causing economic shocks and impacting industries heavily reliant on petroleum products. Energy companies can use scenario analysis to evaluate the potential consequences of such an event, explore alternative energy sources, invest in renewable energy technologies, and diversify their operations to reduce dependence on fossil fuels.

- *Technology Start-up*

  Suppose a technology start-up is developing a new product and faces uncertainties regarding market adoption, competition, and regulatory changes. By conducting scenario analysis, the start-up can create multiple scenarios that explore different market conditions, customer preferences, and competitive landscapes. This analysis helps the start-up identify potential risks, anticipate market shifts, and adjust its business strategy accordingly. For example, scenario analysis might reveal the need for additional investments in research and development, adjusting the product pricing, or exploring new markets.

- *Supply Chain Management*

  Imagine a scenario where a global pandemic disrupts supply chains, causing shortages of critical components and raw materials. Manufacturers heavily reliant on international suppliers' experience production delays, increased costs, and customer dissatisfaction. By conducting scenario analysis, companies can identify vulnerabilities in their supply chains, explore alternative sourcing options, establish strategic stockpiles, or develop contingency plans to ensure business continuity in the face of supply chain disruptions.

- *Environmental Impact*

  Consider a scenario where stricter environmental regulations are implemented, requiring companies to reduce their carbon emissions and adopt sustainable practices. Through scenario analysis, organizations can explore different regulatory frameworks, carbon pricing mechanisms, and market demands for environmentally friendly products. This analysis helps companies anticipate and adapt to future environmental requirements, such as investing in renewable energy, optimizing production processes, or developing eco- friendly products to gain a competitive edge.

In each of these examples, scenario analysis enables organizations to assess the potential impact of various factors, make informed decisions, and develop strategies that enhance resilience and adaptability. By considering multiple scenarios, organizations can proactively manage risks, seize opportunities, and position themselves for success in an uncertain and dynamic business environment.

Throughout the process of risk identification, it is essential to note identified risks in a structured manner, capturing pertinent details such as risk descriptions, potential causes, potential consequences, and their associated sources. This information serves as the foundation for subsequent risk evaluation and analysis.

Risk identification is an ongoing process that should be revisited frequently to account for new threats that may arise as a result of changing conditions. It is crucial to cultivate a risk-aware culture within the organization, urging all stakeholders to remain vigilant and report potential risks as they arise.

Identification of risks is the first stage in effective risk management. By employing a variety of techniques and involving stakeholders, organizations can comprehensively and proactively identify potential risks. This procedure lays the groundwork for subsequent risk evaluation, analysis, and the development of appropriate risk response strategies.

RISK ASSESSMENT

In the realm of risk management, risk assessment is a crucial procedure involving the identification, evaluation, and prioritization of potential risks to determine their likelihood and potential impact. It serves as the foundation for effective risk management strategies, allowing individuals and organizations to make informed decisions and allocate resources to mitigate or address risks appropriately.

The primary objective of risk assessment is to analyze and quantify risks systematically in order to comprehend their nature, severity, and potential consequences. This procedure includes a few essential stages that aid in identifying and comprehending risks comprehensively.

Identifying and recognizing the potential hazards an organization or project may face is the initial step in risk assessment. This requires a comprehensive analysis of internal and external factors, such as processes, systems, stakeholders, industry trends, and regulatory requirements. Techniques for identifying risks, such as ideation, checklists, and historical data analysis, are frequently used to identify a wide variety of risks.

Risk analysis is an important part of the risk management process since it involves identifying and evaluating potential hazards to determine their likelihood and impact. It assists organizations in risk prioritization and making informed decisions about risk treatment and mitigation measures. Depending on the complexity and availability of data, risk analysis can be done qualitatively or quantitatively. Let us take a closer look at risk analysis with some examples:

Qualitative Risk Analysis

This is a subjective assessment of hazards based on their features and impact. It does not rely on numerical data to assess hazards, instead employing descriptive scales. The following are some examples of qualitative risk analysis techniques.

- *Risk Probability and Impact Assessment*

  In this technique, subjective probabilities and impact levels are assigned to detected risks. Based on their experience and knowledge, a project manager might grade the likelihood of a project delay as "high" and the impact as "moderate."

- *Risk categorization*

  Risks are classified according to their nature or source, for example, financial risks, operational risks, technological risks, or legal risks. Categorization aids in comprehending the many sorts of hazards and their possible impact on various elements of the company.

- *Risk Scoring*

  Risk scoring entails assigning risk scores or ratings based on predetermined criteria. A risk matrix, for example, can be used to classify hazards as low, medium, or high depending on their likelihood and impact. This enables organizations to prioritize hazards for future investigation and mitigation.

Quantitative Risk Analysis

Quantitative risk analysis is a more objective, data-driven approach to risk assessment. It quantifies the likelihood and potential impact of hazards using numerical data and statistical methodologies. Among the quantitative risk analysis approaches are as follows.

- *Monte Carlo Method*

  Monte Carlo simulation is the process of performing many simulations based on probabilistic inputs in order to examine the range of possible outcomes and their associated probabilities. It is frequently used in financial risk analysis to evaluate investment portfolios, pricing models, and project timelines.

- *Sensitivity Analysis*

  The influence of modifying input factors on the overall outcome or outcomes is assessed using sensitivity analysis. It aids in identifying the most crucial variables that have a major impact on risk exposure. In a manufacturing process, for example, sensitivity analysis can quantify the impact of differences in raw material costs on project profitability.

- *Expected Monetary Value (EMV) Analysis*

  The expected value of each risk event is calculated using EMV analysis by multiplying the likelihood of occurrence by the related impact or cost. It enables businesses to prioritize risks based on their potential financial impact and identify the most cost- effective risk mitigation methods.

As an example, consider a construction job. The project team evaluates potential hazards during the risk analysis phase, such as severe weather conditions, labor shortages, design revisions, and material price fluctuations. The team then uses qualitative or quantitative methodologies to analyze the likelihood and impact of each risk.

For qualitative analysis, the team might rank the possibility of poor weather conditions as "medium" and the impact as "high" because it can cause project delays and cost increases. Similarly, the team may rank labor shortages as "low" but having a "high" impact because they can reduce productivity and increase overtime expenses.

The team may utilize previous weather data to determine the risk of poor weather conditions and estimate the cost of delay for quantitative analysis. They may also examine past labor market trends to assess the possibility of labor shortages and the financial implications.

The project team can prioritize risks, build contingency plans, allocate resources, and make informed judgments on risk treatment tactics such as contractual agreements, schedule buffers, or alternate sourcing possibilities based on the risk analysis findings.

Remember that risk analysis provides useful insights into prospective risks, helping organizations to better manage resources, prepare contingencies, and make proactive actions to reduce the impact of uncertainty.

Risk Evaluation

A key component of risk management is risk evaluation, which is evaluating and classifying hazards according to their importance and likelihood of occurring in order to assign them a priority. It seeks to give a thorough understanding of the hazards discovered during the risk assessment phase and empowers businesses to decide on effective risk management and mitigation techniques.

The following essential factors are considered while evaluating risks:

- Risk Severity: This term describes the possible effects or impact that a risk occurrence could have on the goals, operations, assets, or reputation of an organization. Normally, risks are rated on a qualitative or quantitative scale, considering things like monetary loss, safety risks, potential legal or regulatory repercussions, operational interruptions, and reputational harm.

- Risk Likelihood: This term describes the likelihood or regularity of a risk event happening. To calculate the possibility of risks, historical data, expert opinions, statistical models, or other pertinent sources of information are analyzed. A qualitative or quantitative scale, ranging from low to high or from rare to regular, is typically used to rate likelihood.

- Risk Tolerance: The ability of a stakeholder or organization to accept or tolerate a particular level of risk. It demonstrates the organization's tolerance for risk and establishes the acceptable degree of exposure to various dangers. The organization's aims, sector, legal constraints, and other contextual elements may all influence risk tolerance.

- Risk Prioritization: After hazards are ranked according to their likelihood and seriousness, they are prioritized to determine how best to deal with them. The highest priority risks are often those with a high probability of occurrence and necessitate quick attention and mitigation strategies. Prioritization aids in efficient resource allocation and concentrates attention on the most important risks that carry the greatest potential for harm or impact.

- Risk Assessment Methodologies: Depending on the type of risk and the information at hand, many approaches can be used to undertake risk evaluation. Risks are given subjective values or scores using qualitative risk assessment techniques like risk matrices or risk scoring based on their significance and likelihood. On the other side, quantitative risk assessment techniques entail employing statistical models, simulations, or calculations to calculate the numerical probabilities and potential economic effects of hazards.

In general, risk evaluation offers a methodical and structured way to comprehending the significance of risks, enabling firms to effectively allocate resources, and put into place risk management procedures. By considering the possible outcomes and likelihood of risks, aligning them with the organization's risk tolerance and objectives, and assuring a proactive approach to risk management, it facilitates decision-making.

Risk Treatment

Risk treatment, also known as risk response, is an important element in risk management. It entails choosing and implementing methods to address identified risks and their potential consequences. Risk management seeks to reduce or eliminate risks, transfer, or share risks with other parties, accept risks within established tolerances, or avoid risks entirely. Risk treatment's goal is to lessen the frequency and severity of negative consequences linked with identified risks.

In risk management, four basic tactics are typically used:

- Risk Avoidance: This method entails taking purposeful steps to remove or prevent dangers. It could include avoiding some activities, stopping processes or projects, or rejecting chances that pose too many risks. Risk avoidance is commonly used when the possible negative consequences of a risk outweigh the benefits or when suitable alternatives are available.

- Risk Reduction or Mitigation: Risk reduction or mitigation is the proactive use of actions to reduce the chance or impact of identified risks. The goal of this technique is to regulate and reduce the occurrence and severity of risks. adopting safety measures, performing regular inspections and maintenance, improving security protocols, adopting redundancy measures, or adding controls and safeguards are all examples of risk mitigation tactics. The goal is to lower the likelihood of a risk event occurring or to reduce the effect of an event that does occur.

- Risk Transfer: Risk transfer entails transferring some or all the risks to another party, generally through contracts or insurance arrangements. Organizations or individuals can protect themselves from any financial or operational losses connected with a risk event by shifting the risk. Purchasing insurance policies, outsourcing tasks to other parties, or entering into agreements that assign responsibility for specific risks to other entities are all examples of risk transfer.

- Risk Acceptance: Risk acceptance is a method that involves deliberately acknowledging and enduring the potential consequences of risks without taking explicit steps to mitigate them. When the costs of risk treatment outweigh the possible benefits, or when the possibility or impact of a risk is assessed to be within tolerable bounds, this technique is often used. Accepting risks does not imply ignoring them, but rather making an informed decision to manage and monitor them within established parameters.

It is crucial to highlight that risk management strategies are not mutually exclusive, and a variety of strategies may be used based on the nature of the risks and organizational objectives. The selection of effective risk treatment solutions necessitates a thorough examination of the risks' possible consequences, available resources, risk appetite, and organizational restrictions.

Effective risk treatment requires continual monitoring and frequent review to ensure that the chosen solutions remain relevant and successful in the changing risk landscape. Organizations may increase their resilience, preserve their assets, and make educated decisions that balance risk and reward by employing appropriate risk management practices.

Risk Monitoring and Evaluation

Risk assessment is a continuous process requiring ongoing surveillance and evaluation. Risks are dynamic and subject to change over time as a result of factors such as market conditions, technological advances, and regulatory modifications. Regular monitoring and review aid in the identification of new risks, the evaluation of the efficacy of implemented risk remedies, and the adjustment of risk management strategies as necessary. By remaining proactive and vigilant, organizations can maintain a robust risk management framework and adapt to emergent risks.

Effective risk assessment necessitates a multidisciplinary approach incorporating collaboration between diverse stakeholders, such as risk managers, subject matter experts, project managers, and senior management. It makes well-informed decisions based on accurate and trustworthy data, informed analysis, and sound judgment.

By conducting comprehensive risk assessments, organizations can anticipate potential threats and opportunities, manage uncertainties proactively, and improve their ability to achieve goals while minimizing the negative impact of risks. In strategic planning, project management, compliance, and overall business resiliency, risk assessment is a crucial tool.

Risk assessment is a fundamental risk management process that allows individuals and organizations to comprehend, evaluate, and rank risks. It enables the development of effective risk mitigation strategies and the making of informed decisions. By adopting a systematic and structured risk assessment methodology, organizations can confidently navigate uncertainty and nurture a culture of resilience and adaptability.

Here are a few examples to illustrate risk monitoring and evaluation in different contexts:

- *Project Risk Monitoring and Evaluation*

  Risk monitoring in a construction project entails regularly tracking and assessing numerous project risks, such as material delivery delays, unfavorable weather conditions, or contractor performance concerns. A risk register can be used by project managers to record and monitor risks throughout the project's lifecycle. They can discover prospective risks that have formed or evolved through monitoring, update risk likelihood and impact estimates, and take the appropriate actions to successfully reduce or respond to the risks.

- *Financial Risk Monitoring and Evaluation*

  To preserve stability and compliance, financial institutions regularly monitor and evaluate financial risks. A bank, for example, may monitor the credit risks connected with its lending portfolio. They review borrowers' creditworthiness on a regular basis, watch changes in economic conditions, and analyze the probable impact on loan defaults. Banks might change their lending procedures, create risk mitigation methods, or designate additional provisions for probable losses by monitoring these risks.

- *Operational Risk Monitoring and Evaluation*

  To maintain smooth and effective operations, a manufacturing organization may monitor and evaluate operational risks. This could entail keeping an eye out for risks such as equipment failure, supply chain interruptions, or process inefficiencies. Regular reviews allow the organization to discover areas for improvement, adopt preventive maintenance measures, and improve process controls in order to eliminate potential risks and optimize operational performance.

- *Information Security Risk Monitoring and Evaluation*

  Organizations monitor and analyze risks in the field of information security in order to safeguard their data and systems against cyber threats. This includes monitoring network traffic in real-time, conducting vulnerability assessments, and reviewing security incident reports. Organizations can use evaluation to identify potential security flaws, assess the effectiveness of existing security measures, and take proactive steps to address vulnerabilities, such as implementing stronger access controls, updating software patches, or providing employee cybersecurity best practices training.

CHAPTER 3

Risk Prioritization and Mitigation

RISK PRIORITIZATION

Risk prioritization is an important part of good risk management since it guides decision- making processes. Organizations face multiple risks in today's complex and uncertain business environment, and it is critical to deploy resources efficiently to handle the most significant threats and opportunities.

Risk prioritization entails assessing and rating risks based on their possible impact and likelihood, allowing companies to focus their resources on the most important issues. Organizations can allocate resources, establish appropriate risk response plans, and adopt mitigation measures to lower the chance and effect of bad events by prioritizing risks.

There are many factors that influence risk prioritization, including,

Impact

A fundamental consideration in risk prioritization is the potential impact or repercussions of a risk. Risks that have the potential to cause considerable injury, financial loss, or disruption to vital activities are usually prioritized. The financial, reputational, environmental, and operational effects can all be measured. Let us consider a manufacturing company that is significantly reliant on a single source for a vital raw material utilized in their manufacturing process. The company recognizes a danger relating to the supplier's financial stability. If the supplier went bankrupt or experienced substantial financial difficulties, there would be a shortage of the raw material, disrupting production and perhaps inflicting significant financial losses for the company.

In terms of impact, the repercussions of this risk can include:

- Financial Loss: As a result of the production standstill and inability to fulfill customer orders, the company may suffer significant financial losses. This could include missed revenue, contract breach fines, and additional costs involved with finding a replacement supplier or reducing the impact.

- Reputational Damage: Failure to meet client requests owing to raw material shortages may result in discontent, unfavorable reviews, and reputational harm. This can result in the loss of existing clients as well as difficulty recruiting new ones.

- Operational Disruption: A supply chain disruption can have a domino impact on the company's operations. Inefficiencies, delays, and challenges in meeting production schedules may result, potentially harming other suppliers, employees, and overall corporate performance.

- Market Share Loss: Prolonged production disruptions can allow competitors to grab market share that the company is unable to supply. This can have long-term consequences for the company's market position and revenue.

The impact of this risk would be rated severe given the probable severity of these consequences. As a result, the risk is likely to be prioritized for immediate attention and risk mitigation steps such as preparing contingency plans, diversifying suppliers, or establishing alternate sourcing possibilities.

Organizations may effectively allocate resources and focus on resolving the risks that have the greatest potential to cause severe harm or disruption by evaluating the impact of risks. This strategy provides proactive risk management and contributes to the organization's resilience and sustainability.

Likelihood

Another important consideration in risk prioritizing is the possibility or probability of a risk occurring. Risks that are more likely to occur are frequently prioritized more promptly because they provide a bigger immediate threat. Historical data, expert judgment, statistical analysis, or predictive algorithms can all be used to determine probability.

Assume you are a risk manager for a company that manufactures electronic equipment. One of the risks you are evaluating is the possibility of a supply chain disruption caused by a natural disaster. You evaluate historical data, expert opinions, and current environmental conditions to determine the likelihood. You discover that the region in which your key suppliers are located is prone to earthquakes and has previously undergone numerous large seismic disasters.

Based on this information, you anticipate that an earthquake will cause a moderate to high supply chain disruption during the next five years. This disruption could result in production delays, revenue loss, and reputational harm.

You rate this risk as high due to the enormous impact such a disruption could have on your firm. You devote resources to developing contingency plans, such as finding alternative suppliers, creating supply chain redundancy, and enhancing communication links with suppliers, in order to assist speedy recovery in the case of an earthquake.

The chance of a supply chain disruption caused by an earthquake affects risk prioritization in this example. Risk management prioritizes this risk over others due to the potential impact of the risk and the moderate to high frequency of occurrence. By focusing resources on minimizing this risk, the business is better equipped to respond to and mitigate the effects of a potential supply chain disruption.

It is crucial to highlight that likelihood estimates are subjective and should be based on the most up-to-date facts and knowledge available. Changes in the environment, technology, or industry factors that may influence the risk landscape should be reviewed and reassessed on a regular basis.

Vulnerability

An important consideration is an organization's or system's vulnerability to a certain risk. Risks that exploit existing vulnerabilities or flaws in controls and safeguards may be prioritized higher because they are more likely to cause harm. Understanding the organization's infrastructure, operations, and security measures is required for assessing vulnerabilities.

Consider a multinational organization that relies significantly on its IT infrastructure to hold sensitive customer data, manage financial transactions, and support vital business activities. In this scenario, the vulnerability could be characterized as a lack of adequate cybersecurity protections within the organization's network.

Factors that may lead to this vulnerability include:

- Outdated Software: The Company may be employing obsolete software or operating systems that are no longer receiving security updates or fixes. This exposes the network to known exploits and malware assaults.

- Weak Password Policies: The organization's password regulations may be lax, allowing employees to use passwords that are easily guessable or regularly used. This raises the possibility of unauthorized access to critical data and systems.

- Insufficient Employee Training: Employees may not receive proper cybersecurity best practices training, such as recognizing phishing emails, avoiding dubious websites, or securely handling sensitive information. This lack of awareness raises the possibility of human error resulting in security breaches.

- Inadequate Firewall and Intrusion Detection Systems: The organization's firewalls and intrusion detection systems may be obsolete or inadequately configured, making it simpler for hackers to obtain unauthorized access to the network or exploit system vulnerabilities.

- Lack of Regular Security Assessments: The organization may not perform regular security assessments or penetration testing to uncover vulnerabilities and flaws in its network architecture. Because of this lack of proactive assessment, potential vulnerabilities are undiscovered and neglected.

- Third-Party Dependencies: The firm may rely extensively on third-party vendors or suppliers for a variety of IT services, such as cloud storage or software solutions. If these suppliers' security efforts are poor, it presents new vulnerabilities that can be exploited.

The presence of these vulnerabilities raises the organization's vulnerability to cyber threats such as data breaches, ransomware attacks, and unauthorized access to critical information. As a result, prioritizing vulnerability mitigation becomes critical in the risk management process. The organization may invest resources to address each vulnerability, such as adopting software updates, enforcing strong password regulations, conducting employee training programs, improving network security measures, and monitoring the efficiency of their cybersecurity safeguards on a regular basis.

Organizations may enhance their defenses, minimize the risk and effect of possible cyber assaults, and secure their vital assets and operations by detecting and fixing vulnerabilities.

Strategic Alignment

Prioritization should be in line with the strategic aims and objectives of the firm. Risks that have a direct influence on achieving strategic objectives or are directly related to important business processes should be prioritized. This guarantees that risk management efforts are directed at safeguarding the organization's critical interests and priorities.

Consider the imaginary XYZ Corporation, which operates in the technology business. Several strategic goals have been defined by the corporation, including increasing market share, expanding into new areas, and improving customer happiness. XYZ Corporation considers the following scenario to link risk priority with these strategic goals:

- Market Share: Increasing XYZ Corporation's market share is one of its strategic aims. Risks that could directly affect market share, such as severe competition, disruptive technologies, or poor customer reviews, would be given higher importance in risk prioritization. XYZ Corporation guarantees that its efforts are aimed on safeguarding and improving its market position by focusing on these risks.

- New Market Expansion: Expansion into new markets is another strategic goal. To ensure a seamless and effective expansion, risks connected with market entry, such as regulatory compliance, cultural diversity, or geopolitical instability, would be prioritized. By proactively addressing these risks, XYZ Corporation may reduce potential roadblocks and increase its chances of effectively entering new markets.

- Customer Satisfaction: XYZ Corporation places a high value on customer satisfaction. Risks that potentially have an influence on consumer satisfaction, such as product quality issues, service disruptions, or data breaches, would be prioritized higher. By focusing on these risks, the company hopes to safeguard its reputation, keep customers loyal, and ultimately achieve its strategic goal of increasing customer satisfaction.

In this instance, XYZ Corporation's risk prioritizing is aligned with its strategic goals. The organization ensures that its risk management efforts are directed toward defending its strategic interests by identifying and prioritizing risks that have a direct influence on market share, new market expansion, and customer satisfaction. This strategic alignment enables XYZ Corporation to effectively manage resources and make informed decisions to mitigate the most essential risks while supporting its long-term business objectives.

It should be noted that the specific strategic alignment criteria and priorities may differ based on the business, industry, and market conditions. Each organization's risk prioritization strategy should be tailored to its own strategic goals and objectives.

Regulatory and Legal Requirements

Compliance with regulatory and legal requirements is an important factor to consider when prioritizing risks. To ensure compliance with applicable rules and regulations, risks that could result in noncompliance, legal obligations, or regulatory punishments are often prioritized. This is especially true in areas with strict regulatory frameworks, such as finance, healthcare, and energy.

Here are some examples of regulatory requirements:

- Anti-Money Laundering (AML) Regulations: To avoid money laundering and terrorist financing, financial institutions must apply stringent AML measures. This includes performing customer due diligence, monitoring transactions, and reporting questionable activity to regulatory authorities.

- Know Your Customer (KYC) Requirements: To reduce the risk of fraud, identity theft, and financial crimes, financial institutions must verify and document the identification of their customers. KYC procedures entail gathering data such as identification documents, proof of address, and beneficial ownership information.

- Data Protection and Privacy Laws: To maintain the confidentiality and security of client information, financial institutions must follow data protection and privacy laws. Obtaining consent for data gathering, establishing proper safeguards, and giving persons control over their personal data are all part of this.

- Securities Regulations: Securities regulations govern the issuance, trading, and disclosure of financial market securities. These rules are intended to safeguard investors, ensure fair and transparent markets, and prohibit fraudulent activity. Registration, reporting, and disclosure obligations are all part of complying with securities legislation.

- Consumer Protection Laws: To protect the interests of clients, financial institutions are subject to consumer protection legislation. These regulations govern activities such as fair lending, term and cost information, and the processing of consumer complaints. Consumer protection laws assist to ensure equitable treatment of customers and the prevention of abusive behavior.

- Sarbanes-Oxley Act (SOX): The SOX Act governs financial reporting, internal controls, and corporate governance for publicly traded firms. It seeks to improve openness, accountability, and integrity in financial reporting in order to safeguard investors and restore public trust in financial markets.

- Payment Card Industry Data Security Standard (PCI DSS): PCI DSS is a set of security rules that govern payment card data protection. It applies to institutions such as banks, retailers, and payment processors that handle cardholder information. PCI DSS compliance aids in the prevention of payment card fraud and data breaches.

- Basel III is a global banking regulatory framework that establishes minimum capital requirements, liquidity norms, and risk management principles. By addressing vulnerabilities discovered during the 2008 financial crisis, it attempts to increase bank resilience and promote financial stability.

These are only a few instances of financial industry regulatory and legal requirements. Organizations in this sector must be knowledgeable about the unique legislation that apply to their area and ensure compliance to avoid legal ramifications, reputational loss, and financial penalties.

Stakeholder concerns

Stakeholder concerns and priorities might impact risk prioritization. Customers, employees, investors, regulatory organizations, and the general public are all examples of stakeholders. Risks that are of particular concern to stakeholders, such as those harming public safety or the environment, may be prioritized in order to retain stakeholder trust and confidence.

- Customers: Customers are an important stakeholder group for any business. Customer safety, product quality, data security, and privacy concerns can all have a substantial impact on risk prioritizing. To ensure customer happiness and loyalty, risks that have the potential to harm customers, undermine their trust or result in unsatisfied experiences may be prioritized.

- Employees: Organizations place a high value on employee well-being and safety. Workplace dangers, occupational health and safety, harassment, discrimination, or insufficient training can all have a negative influence on employee morale and productivity. To safeguard the workers and preserve a pleasant work environment, such risks may be prioritized.

- Investors: Investors and shareholders are worried about an organization's financial stability and profitability. Market instability, economic downturns, supply chain disruptions, and regulatory changes, for example, may be prioritized to protect investor interests and retain shareholder value.

- Regulatory Bodies: Organizations operating in regulated environments must comply with laws, regulations, and industry standards. Risks that could result in noncompliance, legal action, or penalties may be prioritized to ensure regulatory compliance and a strong relationship with regulatory agencies.

- Local Communities: Organizations that operate in specific geographical areas owe it to local communities to consider their concerns. To address community concerns and maintain a positive reputation in the local region, risks with possible repercussions on the environment, public health, or community well-being may be prioritized.

- Suppliers and Partners: Organizations rely on suppliers and partners to keep their operations running smoothly. Supply chain disruptions, vendor dependability, and contractual commitments can all have an impact on an organization's capacity to deliver products or services. Prioritizing risks affecting the organization's core suppliers or key partners aids in ensuring continuity and minimizing disruptions.

- Public and Media: Public perception and media coverage can have a substantial impact on an organization's reputation and brand image. To safeguard the organization's image and retain public trust, risks that have the potential to draw unwanted attention, damage the brand's reputation, or provoke public uproar may be prioritized.

When prioritizing risks, firms must engage stakeholders proactively, understand their issues, and weigh their opinions. Organizations can develop trust, strengthen relationships, and improve their entire risk management strategy by addressing stakeholder concerns.

Available resources

The availability of resources, such as finance, manpower, and time, can also have an impact on risk prioritizing. Organizations must examine their ability to effectively handle and reduce risks. Risks that may be addressed with existing resources or through cost- effective solutions may be prioritized higher, but risks that need significant resources may be prioritized differently.

Consider a manufacturing corporation that wants to prioritize risks in their manufacturing process. In this situation, available resources could include:

- Budget: The Company's budget for risk management operations is restricted. Risks that may be addressed within the specified budget may be prioritized higher since they can be mitigated without exceeding budgetary restrictions. Risks requiring large financial expenditure, on the other hand, may be deprioritized or demand further explanation.

- Personnel: A risk management team is in place at the organization. Personnel availability and expertise can have an impact on risk prioritizing. Risks that are aligned with the team's abilities and experience can be addressed more effectively, but risks that require specialist knowledge or additional manpower may be prioritized lower or require external assistance.

- Time: Time is a valuable resource for dealing with dangers. Risks that constitute an immediate threat or have a greater potential impact in a short period of time may be prioritized for quick action. Dangers with longer-term repercussions or dangers that may be addressed over a longer timeframe, on the other hand, may be prioritized differently, considering the urgency of other risks.

- Technology and Infrastructure: The technological capabilities and infrastructure of the organization influence risk prioritization. Risks that may be handled using existing technology solutions or infrastructure may be prioritized since they can be executed with minimal effort. Risks that necessitate significant upgrades or infrastructure improvements may be reprioritized or necessitate a longer-term plan.

- External Support: The availability of external assistance, such as consultants or specialist service providers, might influence risk prioritizing. Risks that necessitate the use of outside expertise or resources may be prioritized based on the availability and cost-effectiveness of such assistance. The corporation may choose to devote resources to hazards that can be effectively addressed with outside help.

In this instance, the manufacturing organization must prioritize risks based on its available resources. They may choose to prioritize risks based on their budget, personnel capabilities, time restrictions, available technology, and infrastructure. By efficiently employing its current resources, the organization may focus on tackling the most significant issues while optimizing its risk management efforts.

It is vital to recognize that resource availability may change over time, and businesses should frequently examine and adapt their risk priority depending on the dynamic resource situation.

Emerging Risks

Effective risk management requires anticipating and resolving new hazards. Risks on the horizon or with the potential to evolve quickly may be prioritized to guarantee early detection and proactive mitigation. In a continually changing world, this enables firms to stay ahead of new dangers and grasp opportunities.

- Cybersecurity and Data Breaches: As technology progresses, cyber threats and data breaches evolve and become more sophisticated. New forms of malware, ransomware attacks, targeted hacking strategies and vulnerabilities in developing technologies such as Internet of Things (IoT) devices and cloud computing are among the rising concerns in this arena. These risks can result in major financial losses, damage to one's reputation, and the compromise of important customer or business data.

- Artificial Intelligence (AI) and Automation: Rapid AI, machine learning, and automation use bring both benefits and hazards. The ethical implications of AI decision- making, algorithm biases, employment displacement, and the possibility for AI systems to malfunction or be exploited are all emerging issues. To enable ethical AI use and to prevent any unforeseen repercussions, organizations must carefully traverse these risks.

- Climate Change and Environmental Risks: Climate change and the risks linked with it are receiving more attention. Extreme weather events, increasing sea levels, resource scarcity, and regulatory reforms aimed at lowering carbon emissions are all emerging dangers. These hazards can have an impact on a variety of industries, including agriculture, real estate, insurance, and energy, and may necessitate firms adapting their operations, supply networks, and business models.

- Geopolitical Uncertainty: Political and geopolitical events can generate new risks that have an influence on global businesses. Trade disputes, economic penalties, geopolitical wars, changes in government legislation, and political instability in certain regions are examples of such hazards. International organizations must monitor and assess these risks in order to secure their operations, investments, and supply networks.

- Technological Disruptions: Rapid technological breakthroughs can disrupt entire businesses and introduce new hazards. Blockchain technology, for example, has the potential to disrupt existing financial systems, while autonomous vehicles offer hazards to the transportation industry. To remain competitive and resilient, organizations must stay on top of technology upheavals and proactively manage the risks that come with them.

- Pandemics and Health crisis: The recent COVID-19 pandemic showed the global health crisis' influence on organizations around the world. The possibility for new infectious diseases, antibiotic resistance, and the weaknesses of global supply chains and transport networks are all emerging hazards in this field. To limit the effect of future health crises, organizations should build robust contingency plans and crisis response methods.

These instances demonstrate that emergent hazards can arise from a variety of sources and have far-reaching consequences for businesses. Businesses must constantly scan the external world, participate in scenario planning, and undertake risk assessments to identify and prepare for these developing hazards. By doing so, firms may successfully adapt, innovate, and respond to potential disruptions and embrace new possibilities.

It is important to remember that priority criteria may differ depending on the specific setting, industry, and organizational goals. Organizations should develop their own risk prioritizing criteria and weighting depending on their own circumstances and risk appetite.

Organizations can efficiently allocate resources, handle significant risks proactively, and improve overall risk management efforts by considering these variables and adopting a systematic and consistent approach to risk prioritization.

Risk prioritization techniques

To assess and prioritize risks, qualitative approaches rely on subjective judgments and expert opinions. In qualitative assessments, techniques such as risk matrices, risk scoring, and risk classification are widely employed. This strategy ranks hazards based on their characteristics and assists in identifying risks that demand quick action.

Advantages of Qualitative Assessment

When compared to quantitative methods, qualitative assessment is often simpler and easier to understand. It does not necessitate complex computations or specialist data analysis abilities, allowing it to be used by a broader range of stakeholders. This ease of use allows for a faster assessment procedure, which is especially useful when dealing with a high number of hazards.

Qualitative evaluation enables for expert judgment and expertise to be included. This method considers the views and opinions of competent personnel with a thorough understanding of the business, its operations, and the hazards involved. Expert judgment can provide crucial insights that quantitative methods alone may not be able to capture.

Qualitative assessment allows for adaptation to various contexts and risk domains. It can be used in instances when there is a scarcity of data or historical information. It enables the assessment of a wide range of risk factors, including developing hazards or those that are difficult to correctly define.

Qualitative assessment promotes a holistic view of risks by considering a variety of qualitative elements such as the nature of the risk, its core causes, and its repercussions. This larger perspective aids in identifying interrelated hazards, connections, and underlying weaknesses that a strictly numerical study may miss.

There are, however, some potential disadvantages of qualitative evaluation:

Inadequate Precision: One of the key disadvantages of qualitative assessment is the inability to quantify precisely. Without quantifiable data, it can be difficult to compare and prioritize hazards appropriately. When numerous assessors are engaged, this might lead to subjective biases or contradictions.

Qualitative evaluation does not provide the amount of information and precision that quantitative methods do. It may not detect tiny differences in risk levels or allow for exact risk comparisons. This constraint can make it difficult to do advanced risk studies, such as cost-benefit analysis or quantitative risk modeling.

Qualitative evaluation frequently relies on descriptive terminology or qualitative scales that are vulnerable to interpretation. This can make communicating and documenting risk assessments difficult, especially when different stakeholders have varying degrees of understanding or expertise.

Communication ambiguity can have an impact on decision-making and the execution of risk-mitigation methods.

Qualitative assessment is primarily reliant on subjective judgment and qualitative data. It may not make appropriate use of quantitative or historical data provided to the organization. This can lead to missed opportunities to capitalize on data-driven insights, as well as incomplete or skewed risk assessments.

Comparing and prioritizing risks might be difficult without accurate numerical numbers. Qualitative assessments may have difficulty providing a clear evaluation of risks based on their relative importance or probable impact. This can make it difficult to deploy resources efficiently or make sound risk management judgments.

While qualitative risk assessment has limits, it can nevertheless be a useful tool when quantitative data is insufficient or a broader, expert-driven perspective is necessary. It is frequently used in conjunction with quantitative methodologies to provide a more comprehensive knowledge of hazards and to enhance decision-making processes.

Quantitative techniques

Quantitative techniques entail assigning numerical values to hazards using statistical data, models, and calculations. To estimate risks based on their likelihood and potential impact, techniques such as probabilistic modeling, Monte Carlo simulations, and decision trees are utilized. This strategy produces a more objective and quantifiable risk ranking.

Advantages of quantitative techniques

Quantitative methods offer a systematic and impartial method of risk appraisal. They can aid in removing biases and subjectivity that may appear in qualitative evaluations by relying on data and mathematical models. The analysis's credibility and dependability are improved by its objectivity.

Quantitative methods provide accurate and exact measurements and forecasts. Statistical models can compute prospective losses or benefits, measure risks, and predict probabilities. Organizations can distribute resources more efficiently and with more knowledge because of this precision.

Quantitative methods make use of data to offer insights and assist choices. They enable the analysis of big datasets and the discovery of patterns, trends, and correlations that might not be readily apparent using only qualitative techniques. Organizations can recognize potential hazards and take reasoned decisions thanks to this data-driven strategy.

Quantitative methods offer a consistent framework for evaluating risks and comparing them. Risks can be easily compared and prioritized by using numerical values and metrics, which facilitates consistent decision-making across various projects or sectors within an organization.

Quantitative techniques allow for the development of risk models and simulations that may be used to assess the possible impact of various scenarios. For example, Monte Carlo simulations can examine the probability distribution of outcomes and provide a range of probable outcomes, assisting in risk mitigation planning and resource allocation. There are some disadvantages to quantitative techniques, as follows.

Quantitative approaches rely greatly on the availability and quality of data. Data that is inaccurate or incomplete might produce misleading results and faulty analyses. Obtaining trustworthy and relevant data can be difficult, especially for developing threats or complicated systems with limited historical data.

In order to simulate complicated systems or uncertainties, quantitative techniques frequently require assumptions and simplifications. These assumptions have the potential to create biases or mistakes into the analysis. It is necessary to critically assess the assumptions and consider their potential impact on the results.

Quantitative methodologies may overlook essential contextual information and qualitative elements that might influence risk assessments. Human judgment, expert opinions, and qualitative insights can all provide valuable perspectives that quantitative models cannot. It is critical to strike a balance between quantitative and qualitative factors.

Quantitative procedures demand a certain amount of technical competence to implement. Developing and using mathematical models, statistical analysis, and computing approaches can be difficult and time-consuming. To properly apply these strategies, organizations may need to invest in training or seek outside expertise.

Quantitative approaches frequently assume a steady and predictable environment. Risks, on the other hand, are intrinsically unknown and might change over time. Quantitative models may have difficulty accounting for rapidly changing conditions, new hazards, and unanticipated events. It is critical to update and alter quantitative evaluations on a frequent basis to reflect changing risk landscapes.

In conclusion, quantitative methodologies provide useful insights and precision in risk analysis and decision-making. They provide objective and data-driven methodologies that enable firms to estimate risks and effectively allocate resources. However, it is critical to recognize their limits, which include data constraints, simplifications, and the requirement for contextual and qualitative considerations. Integrating quantitative and qualitative assessments can aid in the development of a more comprehensive and rigorous risk management strategy.

Risk Scoring and Ranking

Risk scoring entails assigning risk scores or ratings based on predetermined criteria. Impact, likelihood, time sensitivity, and other relevant characteristics may be included in these criteria. Risks are then scored and ranked, with higher-scoring risks regarded as more severe and requiring quick response.

There are several advantages of Risk Scoring and Ranking:

Risk scoring and ranking give a structured and systematic approach for objectively comparing hazards. It becomes easier to identify and evaluate hazards based on their severity and potential impact by assigning scores or rankings.

These strategies aid in risk prioritization by directing attention and resources toward risks with higher scores or rankings. This enables firms to better manage their limited resources by addressing the most serious threats first. Risk scoring and ranking procedures give a consistent framework for evaluating risks across an organization's many projects, departments, or business units. This consistency encourages consistency in risk management approaches and allows for successful communication and decision-making.

Scoring and ranking make it easier to communicate risks to stakeholders in a clear and succinct manner. Risks can be presented in a more clear and comparable manner using a standardized approach, allowing stakeholders to make informed decisions and take relevant measures.

Organizations can focus their efforts on establishing mitigation solutions for the most significant risks by prioritizing hazards. This proactive approach enables rapid risk response planning and implementation, lowering the frequency and severity of adverse events.

The disadvantages of risk scoring and ranking are as follows:

Methodologies for risk scoring and ranking may add subjectivity to the process. Individual biases or interpretations may influence the assigning of scores or rankings, potentially leading to conflicting findings. To reduce subjectivity, it is critical to set explicit norms and criteria.

Risk scoring and ranking approaches frequently entail the simplification and consolidation of complex risk data. This simplification can result in the loss of essential nuances and details, perhaps neglecting critical aspects of hazards that a scoring or ranking system cannot fully represent.

While risk score and ranking provide a relative comparison, they may not fully reflect quantitative components of risks, such as exact probability or financial impact. The use of discrete scores or ranks may oversimplify the underlying complexity of dangers, making proper assessment difficult.

Scoring and ranking techniques may fail to account for specific contextual aspects that determine risk importance. Different sectors, projects, or organizational cultures may necessitate tailored considerations that go beyond a typical scoring or ranking system.

Risks are not static and can change over time. Scoring and ranking may not represent the dynamic nature of hazards or account for changes in the risk environment appropriately. To guarantee continuing risk management efficacy, scores, and rankings must be reassessed and adjusted on a regular basis.

It is critical to understand that risk scoring and ranking should be utilized as complimentary techniques within a larger risk management framework. They should be used in conjunction with other qualitative and quantitative risk assessment methodologies to ensure a thorough awareness of risks and allow for well-informed decision-making.

Organizations can effectively exploit risk scoring and ranking methods while addressing their inherent inadequacies by acknowledging the benefits and limits of these methods.

Cost-Benefit Analysis

Risks can be prioritized in some situations based on a cost-benefit analysis. This method entails weighing the prospective expenses of addressing a risk against the potential benefits of risk mitigation. Risks with a greater benefit-to-cost ratio are prioritized.

The level of risk that a company is ready to accept in order to achieve its goals is referred to as risk appetite. Organizations can prioritize risks that exceed acceptable thresholds by setting risk appetite and tolerance levels, ensuring that resources are focused on controlling risks that go outside acceptable bounds.

Effective risk prioritizing necessitates a methodical approach that considers many aspects and involves key stakeholders. It is a continuous process that should be assessed and modified on a frequent basis as new risks emerge and existing risks change. By carefully prioritizing risks, organizations may address the most serious threats first, deploy resources more efficiently, and improve their overall risk management procedures.

Risk Mitigation

Risk mitigation is an important part of the risk management process since it tries to lower the likelihood and impact of potential risks on an organization or project. It entails developing and implementing plans, actions, and controls to reduce, eliminate, or transfer risks. Organizations may improve their resilience, safeguard their assets, and raise their chances of success by proactively managing risks.

Effective risk mitigation necessitates a systematic and complete approach that includes risk identification, analysis, evaluation, and response. It entails comprehending the existence and characteristics of risks, assessing their potential repercussions, and devising effective countermeasures.

Key Risk Mitigation Principles

Risk Avoidance

In certain circumstances, avoiding a danger entirely is the most efficient method to reduce it. This entails evaluating potential risks and making strategic decisions to avoid behaviors or situations that could expose the organization to serious hazards. While risk avoidance is not always practicable or practical, it is nonetheless an effective risk reduction approach when viable alternatives exist.

Risk Transfer

The financial or operational weight of risk is transferred to another party through risk transfer. This can be accomplished through a variety of means, including insurance policies, contracts, and outsourcing arrangements. Organizations can decrease their exposure and assign responsibility to parties better able to handle certain risks by shifting risks to external entities.

Risk Reduction

Risk reduction tries to reduce the possibility or impact of risk by applying procedures that target its underlying causes or contributing variables directly. This can include developing safety rules, strengthening security measures, increasing quality control processes, or putting in place redundancy systems. To effectively manage vulnerabilities, risk reduction solutions frequently include investments in resources, technology, training, or infrastructure.

Risk Contingency Planning

Risk contingency planning is creating predetermined reaction strategies that will be implemented when specific risks occur. This method enables companies to predict future scenarios and take action to mitigate the effect of risks when they materialize. In response to specific hazards, contingency plans often include roles and duties, communication protocols, resource allocation, and alternative tactics to be adopted.

Risk Monitoring and Review

Risk reduction is an ongoing process that necessitates constant monitoring and frequent evaluation. Organizations can identify developing risks, evaluate the efficacy of current controls, and adapt their strategy by routinely assessing the effectiveness of applied mitigation measures. This iterative process guarantees that risk reduction initiatives stay relevant and adaptable to changing conditions.

Challenges and Considerations

While risk reduction is critical for organizational resilience, there are various problems and factors to consider:

Trade-offs

Risk-mitigation solutions may include trade-offs such as higher expenses, less flexibility, or lengthier decision-making procedures. To avoid jeopardizing overall performance, it is critical to find a balance between risk reduction and other corporate objectives.

Uncertainty

Risk mitigation necessitates making informed decisions based on available knowledge, which may be ambiguous. Organizations must assess risks based on the best available evidence and keep their understanding up to current when new information becomes available.

Complexity

Organizations operate in complicated contexts with interrelated hazards that can have cascading repercussions. Effective risk mitigation necessitates a comprehensive awareness of these intricacies as well as the capacity to traverse interdependencies across multiple risk categories.

Changing Landscape

The risk landscape is dynamic and ever-changing. Existing hazards might evolve over time, and new risks can emerge. To effectively manage their exposures, organizations must remain watchful, adjust their risk mitigation methods, and anticipate future threats.

Risk mitigation is a critical component of risk management because it helps companies to address possible hazards and defend their interests in advance. Organizations can reduce the likelihood and impact of risks by implementing a variety of measures such as risk avoidance, transfer, reduction, and contingency planning. Risk mitigation needs a thorough awareness of the hazards, ongoing monitoring, and the willingness to react to changing circumstances. Organizations may strengthen their resilience, and decision- making, and develop a culture of risk awareness and preparedness by prioritizing risk mitigation.

CHAPTER 4

Technology and Risk

Technology has become an indispensable aspect of our modern life, affecting the way we live, work, and interact with our surroundings. It includes a wide range of tools, methods, and processes that allow us to complete activities more quickly, communicate instantly across long distances, and access information at our fingertips. However, in addition to the various benefits provided by technology, there are inherent risks that must be understood and controlled in order to ensure its appropriate and safe usage.

Technology is referred to as the application of scientific knowledge and engineering concepts to invent, develop, and deploy tools, gadgets, and systems that expand human capabilities and improve many parts of our life. It includes many different industries, such as information technology, telecommunications, manufacturing, healthcare, transportation, and many more. Technology continues to evolve at an exponential rate, influencing businesses and revolutionizing the way we function as a society, from Smartphone and computers to artificial intelligence, blockchain, and robotics.

While technology can provide enormous benefits and open new doors, it also poses risks that must be properly addressed and handled. These dangers can originate from a variety of sources and can affect individuals, organizations, and even entire communities. Understanding and efficiently managing these risks is critical to ensuring safe and ethical technology use.

Cybersecurity is one of the most serious threats associated with technology. Our reliance on technology increases our exposure to cyber assaults. Malicious actors can obtain unauthorized access, steal sensitive information, disrupt operations, or inflict harm by exploiting flaws in software, networks, and infrastructure. Data breaches, identity theft, ransomware attacks, and the compromising of vital infrastructure are all examples of cybersecurity dangers. To avoid these dangers and safeguard against cyber threats, organizations and people must deploy robust security measures such as encryption, firewalls, and regular system updates.

Privacy and data protection are two more major risks associated with technology. With the increased collection, storage, and sharing of personal information via technology, there is growing concern about data misuse or illegal access. Individuals' rights can be violated and their reputations harmed as a result of privacy infractions. Stricter legislation, such as the General Data Protection Regulation (GDPR) of the European Union and the California Consumer Privacy Act (CCPA), aims to protect personal data and hold corporations accountable for it.

GENERAL DATA PROTECTION REGULATION (GDPR)

The GDPR is a comprehensive data protection law that went into force on May 25, 2018. It applies to all European Union (EU) member states and governs the processing and protection of people' personal data inside the EU. If a company processes the data of EU residents, the GDPR has a substantial impact on how it handles and manages personal data, regardless of its location.

Key Principles of the GDPR

- Lawfulness, Fairness, and Transparency: Personal data must be processed in accordance with the law, fairly, and transparently. Organizations must have a legal basis for processing personal data and give clear and accessible information about the processing activities to individuals.

- Purpose Limitation: Personal data should only be acquired for specific, explicit, and lawful objectives. Organizations must verify that the data is not used for purposes other than those for which it was obtained.

- Data Minimization: The GDPR stresses data minimization, requiring enterprises to acquire and process only the personal data required for the intended purpose. Organizations should avoid collecting excessive or useless data.

- Accuracy: Personal information must be accurate and up to date. Organizations must take reasonable steps to ensure that erroneous or outdated data is corrected or destroyed.

- Storage Limitation: Personal data should be stored in a manner that allows persons to be identified for no longer than is necessary for the indicated purpose. When data is no longer required, organizations must set proper retention periods and delete or anonymize it.

- Integrity and Confidentiality: Organizations must take suitable security measures to prevent unauthorized access, loss, destruction, or manipulation of personal data. They must ensure the data's confidentiality, integrity, and availability.

- Accountability: The GDPR establishes the notion of accountability, which holds enterprises accountable for adhering to the GDPR's standards. This includes putting in place the necessary rules, procedures, and paperwork to demonstrate compliance.

Key Rights of Individuals under the GDPR

- Right to Information: Individuals have the right to be informed about how their personal data is collected, used, and processed.

- Right of Access: Individuals have the right to access their personal information and see how it is being handled.

- Right to Rectification: Individuals can request that erroneous or incomplete personal data be corrected.

- Right to Erasure (Right to be Forgotten): Individuals have the right to have their personal data deleted under specific conditions, such as when the data is no longer required for the original purpose or when the subject withdraws consent.

- Right to Restriction of Processing: Individuals have the right to request that their personal data be restricted from being processed in certain instances, such as when the veracity of the data is questioned.

- Right to Data Portability: Individuals have the right to have their personal data transferred to another data controller in a structured, frequently used, and machine- readable manner.

- Right to Object: Individuals have the right to object to personal data processing, including direct marketing and processing for legitimate interests.

- Right to Withdraw Consent: Individuals have the right to withdraw their consent to personal data processing at any time.

CALIFORNIA CONSUMER PRIVACY ACT (CCPA)

The California Consumer Privacy Act (CCPA) is a landmark privacy law adopted in the state of California, United States, to strengthen California residents' privacy rights and protection. The CCPA was passed into law on June 28, 2018, and it went into effect on January 1, 2020. It has had a considerable impact on both internal and external data privacy practices and policies in California.

Key Features of the CCPA

The CCPA applies to enterprises that collect or sell personal information about California residents who meet specified conditions. The CCPA applies to a firm if its annual gross revenue exceeds a certain threshold, it buys, receives, or sells personal information from a certain number of California residents, or it gets a major amount of its revenue from selling personal information.

- Consumer Rights: The CCPA provides California residents with important personal information privacy protections. These rights include the right to know what personal information is collected and how it is used, the right to access and obtain a copy of their personal information, the right to request deletion of their personal information, the right to opt-out of the sale of their personal information, and the right to not be discriminated against in terms of services or pricing for exercising their privacy rights.

- Business Obligations: The CCPA imposes a variety of requirements on businesses that fall under its purview. Businesses must give consumers clear and visible disclosures regarding their data collection and processing methods, including the objectives for which personal information is acquired and the types of third parties with whom the information is shared. They must also put in place measures that make it easier for consumers to exercise their rights, such as dedicated toll-free numbers or online request forms. Furthermore, firms must put in place appropriate security measures to protect personal information.

- Personal Information selling: The CCPA defines "sale" of personal information as the exchange, transfer, or disclosure of personal information to a third party for monetary or other valuable consideration. It gives consumers the option to refuse the sale of their personal information. To facilitate this, opt-out, businesses must give a clear and noticeable "Do Not Sell My Personal Information" link on their website.

- Enforcement and Penalties: The California Attorney General oversees enforcing the CCPA. Businesses that do not comply may face civil penalties and fines for each infringement. Consumers have the right to sue firms in the event of data breaches caused by a company's failure to establish and maintain reasonable security measures.

- Amendments and CCPA Regulations: Since its inception, the CCPA has been amended to clarify key clauses and address stakeholder concerns. The Attorney General of California has also published regulations to further interpret and execute the CCPA. These regulations provide guidance on several aspects of compliance, such as notice requirements, consumer request verification, and the handling of minors' personal information.

It is worth noting that the CCPA influenced other privacy legislation, both at the state and international levels, like the Virginia Consumer Data Protection Act (CDPA) and the California Privacy Rights Act (CPRA).

The CCPA is a big step forward in privacy regulation, emphasizing consumer rights and giving individuals more control over their personal information. It has forced firms to rethink their data practices, put in place comprehensive privacy measures, and increase openness in the management of personal information.

CANADIAN PRIVACY RULES AND REGULATIONS

In Canada, privacy rules and regulations are principally managed by the Personal Information Protection and Electronic Documents Act (PIPEDA), a federal statute. PIPEDA establishes guidelines for organizations' acquisition, use, and disclosure of personal information during their commercial activities. It is crucial to remember, however, that certain Canadian provinces have their own privacy legislation that applies to enterprises operating within those territories.

Here are key features and provisions of Canadian privacy rules and regulations:

PIPEDA (Personal Information Protection and Electronic Documents Act)

1. *Applicability*
    *   Unless a province has substantially identical law, PIPEDA applies to the collection, use, and disclosure of personal information by private sector entities engaged in commercial activities across Canada.

- It establishes principles and procedures for gaining consent, restricting personal information collection, ensuring data accuracy, securing information, and giving persons with access to their personal data.

2. *Consent*

- The Personal Information Protection and Electronic Documents Act (PIPEDA) highlights the necessity of getting meaningful consent from individuals before collecting, using, or revealing their personal information.

- Consent must be informed, voluntary, and based on clear and reasonable explanations of why the information is being used or shared.

3. *Accountability*

- Organizations are accountable for the personal information under their control and must appoint an individual or individuals to ensure that privacy responsibilities are met.

- They must create and implement policies and procedures to protect personal information, respond to privacy complaints, and educate their employees and consumers about their privacy practices.

4. *Purpose of Collection:*

- Consent for any extra uses or disclosures.

5. *Correction and Access:*

- Individuals have the right, subject to certain limitations, to access their personal information kept by an organization and request adjustments if it is inaccurate or incomplete.

- Access requests must be responded to within a reasonable time limit, and organizations must supply the requested information or explain any denials.

6. *Security and precautions:*
    - Organizations must use suitable security precautions to protect personal information from loss, illegal access, disclosure, copying, alteration, or disposal.
    - The level of security should be proportional to the importance of the information.

7. *Breach Notification:*
    - Organizations must report any breaches of security protections that constitute a real risk of serious harm to the Office of the Privacy Commissioner of Canada and impacted people.

8. *Provincial Privacy Legislation:*
    - Some jurisdictions, such as British Columbia, Alberta, and Quebec, have established their own privacy legislation that applies to enterprises operating within their borders.
    - These provincial regulations may have additional or different requirements than PIPEDA, and organizations operating in those provinces must follow both federal and provincial rules.

Organizations doing business in Canada must get acquainted with the applicable privacy laws and regulations, establish suitable privacy practices, and maintain compliance with the principles and requirements outlined in PIPEDA or comparable provincial legislation. Legal counsel or privacy experts can provide customized advice targeted to an organization's specific circumstances and requirements.

When discussing the risks linked with technology, ethical questions also come into play. As technology progresses, worries regarding its impact on societal values, individual rights, and the possibility of bias or discrimination arise. Ethical quandaries arise in fields such as artificial intelligence, autonomous vehicles, and genetic engineering, where technological decisions might have far-reaching repercussions.

Addressing these ethical hazards and ensuring that technical innovations correspond with social values and enhance human well-being is critical.

ETHICAL QUANDARIES IN ARTIFICIAL INTELLIGENCE

As AI technologies improve and integrate into numerous sectors of society, ethical quandaries in the field of artificial intelligence (AI) have become increasingly prominent. The complexity of AI systems, their potential impact on persons and society, and the lack of defined ethical frameworks have raised several ethical problems and dilemmas. Here are some significant domains in AI where ethical quandaries arise:

AI systems may unintentionally perpetuate biases and discrimination in training data or programming. This can result in discriminatory treatment of specific persons or groups, especially in areas such as hiring, lending, and law enforcement. Addressing prejudice in AI systems and guaranteeing fairness is a key ethical concern.

Privacy and Surveillance: Artificial intelligence (AI) technology such as facial recognition and data analytics raise worries about invasion of privacy and mass surveillance. Balancing the benefits of AI-enabled monitoring with individual privacy rights is a huge ethical quandary, as the risk of abuse and misuse of personal data is a legitimate worry.

AI systems are frequently opaque, making it challenging to comprehend their decision-making processes. This lack of transparency raises concerns about who should be held accountable for AI systems' actions and decisions. Developing procedures for AI algorithm transparency, explainability, and accountability is a significant ethical concern.

The advancement of self-driving cars and autonomous weapons raises concerns about the extent of human control and responsibility. The ethical quandary is establishing when and how humans should retain control over AI systems to guarantee they accord with human values and do not pose unnecessary risks.

As AI technologies become more widely adopted; they have the potential to automate functions that were previously handled by people, resulting in job displacement and economic disruption. The ethical challenge is to address the social and economic consequences of AI-driven automation while also providing a just transition for affected persons and communities.

AI systems are increasingly being charged with making ethical decisions, such as in healthcare, criminal justice, and resource allocation. A significant ethical issue is determining how AI should make ethically sensitive decisions and incorporating ethical considerations into AI systems.

AI is heavily reliant on massive amounts of data. In the context of AI, questions about data ownership, permission, and data governance arise. The ethical problems include assuring responsible data collecting, reducing data breaches, protecting individual rights, and implementing equitable data sharing policies.

Artificial intelligence-powered devices have the ability to manipulate and influence people's behavior, attitudes, and decisions. This raises questions about the ethical limitations of persuasive technology, as well as AI developers' and organizations' obligation to maintain transparency and protect users from undue manipulation.

To address these ethical quandaries, a multi-stakeholder approach encompassing researchers, legislators, industry executives, ethicists, and the general public is required. It is critical to establish ethical principles, rules, and regulations to regulate the development, implementation, and usage of AI. Furthermore, establishing interdisciplinary collaborations and including ethical considerations across the AI system's whole lifecycle can assist ensure that AI technologies are developed and used responsibly and beneficially.

As AI advances, it is vital to have continual dialogues, debates, and critical reflections on AI's ethical implications. By proactively addressing these ethical quandaries, we can try to maximize the potential of AI for society benefit while reducing its negative consequences.

Autonomous car systems rely on AI algorithms educated on massive volumes of data. The algorithms may unintentionally perpetuate biased behavior if the training data contains biases or reflects societal disparities. Concerns have been raised that AI systems may demonstrate racial or gender bias when making choices on the road. It is an ethical duty to address these biases and ensure justice in the design and deployment of autonomous systems.

ETHICAL QUANDARIES IN AUTONOMOUS VEHICLES

Ethical quandaries in the realm of self-driving automobiles highlight the difficult ethical quandaries that arise when artificial intelligence (AI) and machine learning algorithms make vital judgments that can have a negative influence on human life. As autonomous vehicles become more common, the following ethical considerations emerge:

Autonomous vehicles may be forced to make split-second decisions that could endanger passengers, pedestrians, or other vehicles. In an unavoidable accident scenario, for example, should the car prioritize the safety of its occupants over pedestrians? This ethical quandary, known colloquially as the "trolley problem," raises concerns about the value of human life and the role of technology in making life-or-death decisions.

The introduction of self-driving cars raises concerns regarding accountability and liability in the event of an accident or failure. When an autonomous car does harm, who should be held accountable? Should the manufacturer of the car, the software developer, or the human occupant have had limited control or oversight? Resolving these difficulties necessitates careful study of legal frameworks, insurance policies, and duty distribution among many players.

Autonomous vehicles generate and handle massive amounts of data, including real-time location data, driving behaviors, and potentially even passenger behavior. Concerns concerning privacy and surveillance arise as a result of how this data is collected, stored, and used. Ownership and control of this data, as well as the need for transparency and informed consent from users, raise ethical concerns.

The widespread use of self-driving cars has the potential to disrupt industries that rely largely on human drivers, such as trucking and transportation services. While self-driving cars provide benefits such as enhanced efficiency and fewer accidents, the ethical aspect is controlling the societal impact of job displacement and providing a just transition for affected people.

Gaining public trust in self-driving cars is critical to their widespread acceptance. Ethical considerations include assuring transparency in the creation and testing of autonomous systems, as well as providing explicit instructions on how crucial decisions are made. Users and the general public should have access to information on autonomous vehicles' safety, dependability, and ethical framework.

To address these ethical quandaries, engineers, legislators, ethicists, and the general public must work together across disciplines. It is critical to establish clear ethical norms, industry standards, and regulations that enable responsible autonomous vehicle development and deployment. Stakeholders can work to ensure that autonomous vehicles are developed and run in a way that prioritizes safety, justice, transparency, and the well- being of society by actively engaging in ethical conversations and incorporating multiple perspectives.

ETHICAL QUANDARIES IN GENETIC ENGINEERING

In domains such as genetic engineering, where the ability to change and modify the genetic makeup of living organisms poses significant moral and philosophical concerns, ethical quandaries do arise. Here are some significant ethical concerns and quandaries related to genetic engineering:

Genetic engineering is the deliberate modification of an organism's genetic code, allowing scientists to modify traits, create new species, or eliminate undesired qualities. This ability to modify life raises concerns about humans "playing God" by changing the fundamental nature of organisms. Such interventions, critics contend, may violate the sanctity of life, and undermine natural evolutionary processes.

The potential for genetic engineering to improve human capacities and traits raises ethical concerns about the limits of augmentation. Should we utilize genetic engineering to increase physical characteristics, intelligence, or even embryos to eradicate diseases or disabilities? The pursuit of human enhancement may worsen socioeconomic inequities, create a gap between genetically modified and non- modified people, and raise concerns about justice and access to these technologies.

The ethical implications of genetic engineering include informed consent difficulties. When it comes to changing the genetic makeup of people or other organisms, problems of permission and autonomy arise. The consent of future generations is especially difficult in the case of human genetic engineering, because changes made today may have lasting consequences for those who are unable to give agreement at the time of the intervention.

Both at the individual and ecological levels, genetic engineering might have unforeseen repercussions. Modifying creatures' genetic features may result in unanticipated health concerns, genetic illnesses, or ecological changes. As scientists and politicians wrestle with the ambiguity and potential risks connected with new technologies, the long-term impacts of genetic changes and the potential for unforeseen consequences raise ethical challenges.

Concerns have been raised concerning the social and economic imbalances that genetic engineering may cause. If genetic changes become widely available, it may result in a divide between those who can and cannot buy upgrades. This has the potential to exacerbate existing socioeconomic inequities, produce new forms of discrimination, and call into question the concept of equal opportunity.

Genetic engineering can have serious environmental consequences. The introduction of genetically modified organisms into ecosystems has the potential to disturb the natural balance, reduce biodiversity, and endanger ecosystems and non-modified species. Ethical concerns arise in the context of potentially irreversible environmental consequences and the need to preserve the ecosystem's long-term viability.

The question of intellectual property and patents emerges with genetic engineering. Patents on genetically modified organisms and certain genetic sequences raise concerns about the commercialization of living things and resource control. According to critics, these patents restrict access to genetic information and may stifle scientific development and innovation.

Due to the fast evolution of genetic engineering technology, the creation of comprehensive ethical principles and regulatory frameworks has lagged. To ensure that these technologies are used responsibly and ethically, strict oversight, transparent decision-making processes, and public participation are required. Ethical quandaries arise when attempting to strike the proper balance between scientific progress, innovation, and protecting against potential hazards and unforeseen consequences.

Furthermore, technological advancements pose operational risks that firms must manage. These dangers include system breakdowns, technical obsolescence, supply chain disruptions, and data loss. In order to mitigate these operational risks and maintain uninterrupted operations, organizations must build robust risk management strategies that include contingency plans, backup systems, and regular maintenance.

Rapid technological innovation also raises concerns about job displacement and social inequality. Automation and digitalization may result in job losses in particular industries, necessitating employees to adjust their abilities in order to remain relevant in an ever- changing employment market. Furthermore, the digital divide between those with and without access to technology can amplify existing inequities, restricting prospects for underprivileged areas. In order to mitigate these concerns, policies, and actions aiming at bridging this difference and supporting inclusive technical breakthroughs are required.

Technology has become an inseparable part of our lives, transforming how we live and work. While it has many advantages, it also has several hazards that must be understood, controlled, and reduced. Among the various obstacles that come with technological breakthroughs are cybersecurity threats, privacy concerns, ethical considerations, operational risks, and socioeconomic ramifications. We can harness the power of technology while reducing its potential risks by implementing proactive risk management techniques, fostering ethical decision-making, and assuring inclusion, resulting in a safer and more sustainable future.

INTRODUCTION TO TECHNOLOGY RISKS

Technology is important in practically every part of our lives in today's interconnected and computerized society. Technology has become omnipresent, from organizations relying on complicated IT systems to consumers using smartphones and social media sites. However, the benefits of technology are accompanied by inherent hazards that organizations and individuals must be aware of and manage appropriately.

This high-level overview of technology risks seeks to provide a complete overview of the potential risks connected with technology use. It will look at several types of technological risks, their consequences, and the tactics used to reduce them. This introduction will provide you with the essential information to traverse the terrain of technology hazards, whether you are a technology expert, a corporate executive, or simply an individual interested in understanding the possible dangers of technology.

EXAMPLES OF TECHNOLOGY RISKS

Cybersecurity Threats

The number and sophistication of cybersecurity threats have expanded substantially in today's linked society. Malicious acts or events that target computer systems, networks, and data with the purpose to disrupt, damage, or obtain unauthorized access to sensitive information are referred to as cybersecurity threats. Understanding the many sorts of cybersecurity risks is essential for enterprises and people to effectively protect their digital assets. Here are some examples of frequent cybersecurity threats:

- Malware: Malware, short for malicious software, is a broad term that encompasses numerous types of malicious code designed to exploit computer system weaknesses. Viruses, worms, Trojans, ransomware, spyware, and adware are all examples of malware. Malware can infiltrate computers via email attachments, rogue websites, infected downloads, or tainted software. Malware, once deployed, can steal critical information, corrupt files, disrupt operations, and allow unwanted access to systems.

- Phishing and Social Engineering: Phishing is a tactic in which attackers imitate legitimate institutions or organizations in order to trick people into disclosing sensitive information such as login credentials, credit card information, or personal information. To acquire illegal access to systems or sensitive data, social engineering tactics entail psychological manipulation, trust exploitation, or deception of persons. Phishing assaults are frequently carried out using emails, instant messaging, or fraudulent websites.

- Distributed Denial of Service (DDoS) Attacks: DDoS attacks entail flooding a targeted system or network with huge amounts of incoming traffic, rendering it inaccessible to genuine users. Attackers initiate these attacks via networks of compromised computers (botnets). DDoS assaults can disrupt services, inflict financial losses, or function as a distraction to allow other harmful operations to take place.

- Insider Threats: Insider threats are hazards posed by employees who have authorized access to sensitive systems and data. These hazards might develop as a result of malevolent purpose, negligence, or unintentional conduct on the part of workers, contractors, or business partners. Insider risks can result in data breaches, intellectual property theft, unlawful access, or system damage.

- Advanced Persistent Threats (APTs): APTs are sophisticated, covert cyberattacks often carried out by highly trained, well-resourced threat actors. Long-term efforts directed at certain targets, such governmental institutions, or major corporations, are what define Pts. Reconnaissance, first compromise, lateral movement, and data exfiltration are some of the processes that an APT involves. APTs can go unnoticed for long stretches of time, giving attackers the chance to obtain private data or keep a prolonged grip on their target computers.

- Zero-day Exploits: Since the vendor is unaware of the flaws in the software or hardware they are targeting, there are no fixes or security upgrades available. Attackers use these flaws to override security measures, run arbitrary code, or gain unauthorized access to systems. Since businesses have no prior knowledge of or defenses against zero- day attacks, they can be very harmful.

- Data Breaches: Data breaches occur when sensitive information, such as personal information, financial information, or intellectual property, is accessed or disclosed without authorization. Cyber attacks, human error, insufficient security measures, or vulnerable systems can all result in breaches. Reputational harm, financial losses, regulatory fines, and legal responsibilities can result from data breaches.

- Ransomware: A particular kind of malware called ransomware encrypts the victim's files and prevents access to them unless a ransom is paid. Organizations can experience severe interruption as a result of ransomware attacks, including the loss of crucial data, operational halts, and monetary expenditures related to ransom payments or recovery operations.

- Supply Chain Attacks: In order to get unauthorized access to target businesses, supply chain attacks compromise the security of dependable suppliers or third-party vendors. Attackers use supply chain flaws, such as hacked software updates or hardware parts, to gain access to systems and networks. Attacks on the supply chain may have far-reaching repercussions because they may affect numerous firms as well as their clients.

- Internet of Things (IoT) Vulnerabilities: IoT device vulnerabilities represent serious cybersecurity dangers as the number of IoT devices, such as connected medical devices, smart home appliances, and industrial control systems, rises. Insecure IoT devices can be used to launch attacks, acquire illegal access, or violate privacy.

It is crucial to remember that cybersecurity risks are always changing and that new threats frequently appear. To reduce the risks brought on by cybersecurity threats, businesses and individuals should keep up with the most recent threat landscape, implement strong security measures, update software and systems frequently, inform users about cybersecurity best practices, and maintain proactive monitoring and incident response capabilities.

RISK MANAGEMENT AND BEST PRACTICES

When it comes to detecting and prioritizing technological risks, businesses use a variety of methodologies and frameworks to ensure a thorough and comprehensive review. These methodologies and frameworks aid in the identification of potential technology-related vulnerabilities, threats, and weaknesses, allowing organizations to deploy resources more efficiently and effectively reduce risks. Here are some regularly used techniques and frameworks:

To identify and prioritize technological risks, organizations frequently rely on established risk assessment procedures. These approaches offer formal frameworks for assessing risks based on criteria like likelihood, impact, vulnerability, and controls. OCTAVE (Operationally Critical Threat, Asset, and Vulnerability Evaluation), NIST SP 800-30, and ISO 31000 are examples of widely used risk assessment approaches.

Threat modeling is a proactive technique to detecting technological risks by assessing potential threats and vulnerabilities in a systematic manner. It entails identifying prospective attack vectors, comprehending existing security mechanisms, and estimating the effect of potential risks. STRIDE (Spoofing, Tampering, Repudiation, Information Disclosure, Denial of Service, Elevation of Privilege) and DREAD (Damage, Reproducibility, Exploitability, Affected Users, Discoverability) threat modeling frameworks aid in assessing and prioritizing threats based on their severity.

Frameworks and methods for vulnerability management are used to identify and prioritize technical risks associated with software, systems, and networks. These frameworks make it easier to find vulnerabilities by using techniques like vulnerability scanning and penetration testing. The Common Vulnerability Scoring System (CVSS) is a vulnerability management methodology that assigns scores to vulnerabilities based on their severity, exploitability, and effect.

Control frameworks like as COBIT (Control Objectives for Information and Related Technologies) and the National Institute of Standards and Technology Cybersecurity Framework give rules and best practices for controlling technology risks. These frameworks aid in the identification of essential technology- related operations, the evaluation of the effectiveness of current controls, and the prioritization of risks based on their potential impact on business objectives and compliance needs.

Risk heat maps depict the prioritizing of technological risks depending on their likelihood and impact. These maps enable stakeholders to immediately understand the relative severity of hazards and make educated decisions. The likelihood of a risk is often shown on one axis and the impact on the other. To depict risk levels, different color-coding or shading is employed, allowing businesses to focus on high-priority risks.

Adherence to industry standards and regulations is a critical component of technology risk management. PCI DSS (Payment Card Industry Data Security Standard) and HIPAA (Health Insurance Portability and Accountability Act) standards, for example, provide principles for identifying and prioritizing technology risks relevant to their respective businesses. Following these guidelines ensures that firms address significant risks while remaining in regulatory compliance.

Organizations use incident and event monitoring systems in real-time to discover and prioritize technology threats. To identify potential risks and anomalies, these systems collect and analyze log data, network traffic, and security events. Organizations can respond quickly to limit risks by correlating and prioritizing events based on their intensity and potential impact.

It is critical for enterprises to take a comprehensive approach to technology risk management, considering a combination of the methodologies and frameworks mentioned above. Organizations can proactively detect, prioritize, and mitigate technological risks by applying these approaches and frameworks, assuring the resilience and security of their systems, data, and operations.

- Cybersecurity Measures: Investigate best practices and tactics for bolstering cybersecurity defenses, including network security, access limits, encryption, regular system updates, and employee awareness training. Recognize the significance of threat intelligence and constant monitoring in recognizing and mitigating cybersecurity risks.

- Data Protection and Privacy Measures: Learn how to protect sensitive data and ensure compliance with privacy rules. Data encryption, data access restrictions, data minimization, consent management, and privacy impact assessments are all topics to be explored.

- Business Continuity Planning: Investigate the significance of business continuity planning in mitigating technological threats. Recognize the importance of data backups, disaster recovery plans, redundancy measures, and incident response protocols in mitigating the effect of system failures or cybersecurity incidents.

STAKEHOLDER ENGAGEMENT AND COLLABORATION

Managing technological risks necessitates collaboration and coordination among multiple stakeholders, such as technology teams, management, legal departments, human resources, and external partners. Recognize the importance of cross-functional collaboration in efficiently detecting, assessing, and managing technological risks.

Technological advancements have changed the business landscape, bringing with them a plethora of new opportunities and benefits. However, as technology advances, organizations confront a variety of technological hazards that can have serious consequences for their operations, data security, and reputation. Regulatory compliance and governance frameworks play an important role in providing advice, standards, and accountability methods to effectively manage these risks. The significance of regulatory compliance and governance frameworks in technical risk management is discussed in this section.

Regulatory compliance refers to adhering to rules, regulations, and industry standards pertaining to technology and data management.

Compliance frameworks assist firms in navigating the complexities of complicated legal obligations such as data protection, privacy rules, intellectual property rights, and cybersecurity standards. Organizations that follow these standards reduce their risk of legal and regulatory penalties while also fostering responsible and ethical behavior.

Governance frameworks enable firms to manage technical risks in an organized manner. They develop standards, rules, and procedures to guide the deployment and management of technological systems and processes. These frameworks frequently contain best practices from the industry, ensuring that firms implement comprehensive risk management techniques and safeguards. Organizations can reduce vulnerabilities and manage potential risks connected with technology use by adhering to these guidelines.

Risk identification and assessment are frequently emphasized as fundamental components of technical risk management in regulatory compliance and governance frameworks. They encourage firms to do thorough risk assessments in order to detect potential risks and assess their potential impact. Organizations may prioritize risks, manage resources effectively, and address vulnerabilities proactively by employing a risk assessment methodology.

Regulatory compliance and governance frameworks provide instructions for applying controls and safeguards to reduce technology risks. Access restrictions, encryption, intrusion detection systems, and incident response protocols are some of the security features that these frameworks help firms implement. Organizations can limit the possibility and impact of technology risks by establishing these measures, protecting their systems and data.

Governance structures encourage accountability and openness in the management of technical risks. They define the roles and responsibilities of stakeholders in technology governance and risk management procedures. This includes delegating risk oversight, monitoring, and reporting tasks. Organizations may promote a culture of risk awareness and encourage timely action to address emerging technological hazards by assuring responsibility.

The need of continuous monitoring and compliance audits is emphasized in regulatory compliance and governance frameworks. Organizations are advised to set up monitoring procedures to track technical hazards, evaluate the effectiveness of control measures, and identify any gaps in compliance. Audits on a regular basis assist firms in identifying flaws, implementing corrective actions, and ensuring continued compliance with rules and governance requirements.

Adapting to an Evolving Technological Landscape: Technology is always evolving, bringing with it new risks and problems. Organizations can react to these developments through regulatory compliance and governance structures. To handle developing risks, they frequently include processes for reviewing and upgrading risk management plans, standards, and controls. This adaptability enables firms to keep up with technological advances while also ensuring the sustainability of their risk management strategies.

Regulatory compliance and governance frameworks are critical in the management of technological risks. They help firms navigate legal and regulatory requirements, establish best practices, identify risks, implement controls, and maintain continuing compliance by providing guidance, standards, and accountability measures. Organizations may effectively address technical risks and secure their operations, data, and reputation in today's quickly expanding technology landscape by incorporating these frameworks into their risk management plans.

FUTURE CHALLENGES AND EMERGING TRENDS

Understanding the hazards associated with technology's use is critical because it has become a vital part of our personal and professional life. You will be better positioned to make educated decisions, protect sensitive information, and navigate the shifting technology landscape if you have a high-level grasp of technology risks, their possible implications, and mitigation techniques.

The way we communicate, work, and engage with the outside world has all been transformed by technology, which has become an essential part of our life. The development of the internet and the growth of artificial intelligence are only two examples of how technology has improved civilization. Along with these developments, there are, nevertheless, risks both now and in the future that should be carefully considered. This in-depth investigation explores the potential dangers and difficulties brought on by technology, both now and in the future.

PRIVACY AND DATA SECURITY

The importance of privacy has increased in the digital age. People run the danger of breaches, identity theft, and privacy invasions as personal data is collected and used more frequently. Threats to cybersecurity, like hacking and data leaks, present serious risks to people, businesses, and even governments. Future cyber threats could be increasingly sophisticated, necessitating strong security measures and increased vigilance to safeguard sensitive data.

AUTOMATION AND JOB DISPLACEMENT

Artificial intelligence and automation are developing quickly, which has the potential to disrupt labor markets and cause job displacement. Certain jobs may become outdated as technology develops, affecting livelihoods and creating socioeconomic difficulties. For the workforce to stay relevant and employable in the future, more automation in a variety of areas may occur.

ETHICAL CONSIDERATIONS IN ARTIFICIAL INTELLIGENCE

Ethical questions surface as artificial intelligence (AI) develops. Bias, accountability, and transparency concerns in AI systems might have unforeseen repercussions and exacerbate already-existing social injustices. The possibility of autonomous weapons, algorithmic discrimination, and the depletion of human decision-making abilities are some of the potential risks of AI in the future.

INFORMATION OVERLOAD AND MISINFORMATION

Information overload and the propagation of false information are the results of the explosion of information through digital platforms. It has been harder and harder to find credible sources among massive volumes of data. Future generations may face greater risks from false information as technology develops, necessitating the development of critical thinking abilities, media literacy, and effective fact-checking systems.

TECHNOLOGICAL DEPENDENCE AND INFRASTRUCTURE VULNERABILITY

Because of our society's increasing reliance on technology, we are more susceptible to disruptions brought on by natural catastrophes, cyberattacks, and system breakdowns. Technology-related failures pose a threat to infrastructure that is necessary for basic services including electricity grids, transportation networks, and communication systems. In order to reduce potential risks and preserve societal stability, it will be essential to ensure the security and resilience of technical infrastructure.

ENVIRONMENTAL IMPACT

Technology not only presents hazards to the environment but also has the capacity to remedy environmental issues. Environmental deterioration is a result of e-waste, energy use, and the carbon footprint connected with technology manufacturing and use. The future risks of technology lay in finding a balance between innovation and environmentally friendly practices in order to reduce our ecological imprint and prevent additional planetary damage.

UNINTENDED CONSEQUENCES OF EMERGING TECHNOLOGIES

There is a chance that new technology will have unintended repercussions. The potential benefits of developments in areas like genetic engineering, nanotechnology, and quantum computing are enormous, but they also bring up issues with biosecurity, ethical boundaries, and unforeseeable threats. To ensure responsible development and usage, emergent technologies must be carefully examined, regulated, and ethical frameworks must be in place.

There is no denying that technology has greatly improved our lives and given us new options. The risks that come along with these breakthroughs, both now and in the future, must be recognized and addressed. We may manage the changing technology landscape more responsibly by being aware of and proactively managing risks related to privacy, employment displacement, ethics, false information, infrastructure vulnerabilities, environmental impact, and upcoming technologies. As we create a future that exploits the advantages of technology while reducing any possible risks, finding a balance between innovation and risk reduction will be essential.

Holding data for ransom has become a common cybercrime method in recent years, posing major hazards to both organizations and individuals.

The Newfoundland and Labrador health care records ransom case is examined in this scenario. This episode highlights the risks of data breaches as well as the consequences of ransomware attacks on vital systems, emphasizing the significance of strong cybersecurity measures.

THE RANSOMWARE OF NEWFOUNDLAND AND LABRADOR HEALTH CARE RECORDS

Cyberattacks are a growing worry for everyone in recent years, and one noteworthy event that has drawn notice is the ransomware attack on Newfoundland and Labrador's medical records. This letter intends to give you a summary of the incident, its ramifications, and the takeaways.

In 2023, a large cyberattack against the Canadian province of Newfoundland and Labrador's healthcare system took place. The network infrastructure was breached by a sophisticated ransomware attack, which exposed countless patients' medical records. A form of malicious software known as ransomware encrypts files and requests a ransom payment in return for the decryption key.

Implications

The breach of Newfoundland and Labrador's medical information had a significant impact on both the patients who were impacted and the healthcare system. Some of the major ramifications are as follows:

- Patient Privacy Breach: The attack affected patients' private and sensitive medical information, perhaps resulting in identity theft and privacy breaches.

- Disruption of Healthcare Services: The attack interfered with healthcare facilities' regular business operations, resulting in delays in patient care, missed appointments, and perhaps dangerous situations for patients.

- Financial Impact: The incident caused the healthcare system to suffer large financial losses due to the cost of recovery, probable legal action, and reputational harm.

- Trust and Reputation: The breach damaged the reputation of both healthcare providers and governmental organizations by undermining public confidence in the healthcare system's capacity to safeguard private data.

Lessons Learned

The ransomware attack on the healthcare records of Newfoundland and Labrador emphasizes the crucial necessity for strong cybersecurity safeguards and proactive risk management techniques. Here are some important things we may take away from this experience:

- Strengthen Cybersecurity Measures: To stop unwanted access to sensitive data, organizations must spend money on sophisticated security systems, such as strong firewalls, intrusion detection systems, and virus protection.

- Regular System Updates and Patches: By installing software updates and patches promptly, vulnerabilities can be fixed and the chance that they will be exploited by hackers is reduced.

- Employee Education and Awareness: Training programs for cybersecurity best practices, like identifying phishing emails, creating strong passwords, and avoiding dubious websites, should be put in place.

- Data Backup and Disaster Recovery Plans: Having strong disaster recovery plans in place and regularly backing up important data can considerably lessen the effects of a ransomware attack.

- Incident Response and Recovery: To ensure a prompt and efficient response to cyber incidents, organizations should create and frequently test incident response procedures. To address the technical, legal, and communication components of an event, a dedicated team must be in place.

- Collaboration and Information Sharing: To bolster defenses and stay current on new threats, government agencies, healthcare institutions, and cybersecurity specialists should cooperate and share information.

- Compliance with Data Protection Regulations: To protect individual privacy and prevent legal repercussions, organizations must abide by pertinent data protection regulations, such as the General Data Protection Regulation (GDPR) or the Personal Information Protection and Electronic Documents Act (PIPEDA) in Canada.

The ransomware attack on the healthcare records of Newfoundland and Labrador serves as a sharp reminder of the threat faced by cybercriminals, which is on the rise. It highlights the urgent need for ongoing development of risk management, incident response, and cybersecurity strategies. Organizations may strengthen their resistance to cyberthreats and safeguard sensitive data by putting in place strong security measures and encouraging a culture of alertness.

Remember that everyone is responsible for cybersecurity, and that by being aware of the effects of such assaults, we can all help create a more secure online environment.

IMPLICATIONS AND CONSEQUENCES

Patient Privacy Breach

Because the stolen health care data contained sensitive personal information such as medical history, test results, and personal identifiers, the hack resulted in a substantial breach of patient privacy. Such breaches have serious consequences for individuals, as they can lead to identity theft, fraud, and other hostile behaviors. Trust in the health-care system can also deteriorate considerably, hurting patient confidence and overall care quality.

Disruption of Health Care Services

The ransomware outbreak severely disrupted health-care services. Accessing patient records, arranging appointments, and providing timely care were all issues for hospitals and clinics. Medical practitioners were forced to rely on manual processes and limited information, which resulted in delays, inefficiencies, and significant patient safety hazards. In the wake of cyber threats, the incident emphasized the vital necessity for robust backup systems and contingency preparations.

Financial Costs and Reputational Damage

Dealing with a ransomware attack cost impacted organizations a lot of money. Aside from the ransom demand, there are costs connected with incident response, system restoration, cybersecurity enhancements, and potential legal action. The tragedy also harmed the health-care system's reputation, affecting public trust, stakeholder confidence, and partnerships with other organizations and countries.

The ransomware attack on Newfoundland and Labrador health care records emphasizes the significance of proactive cybersecurity measures and risk mitigation tactics. This incident taught us several important lessons, including:

Robust Cybersecurity Infrastructure

Organizations must create and maintain a strong cybersecurity infrastructure, which includes firewalls, intrusion detection systems, encryption methods, and security updates that are up to date. Regular vulnerability assessments and penetration testing can assist in identifying and correcting potential system flaws.

Employee Training and Awareness

Cybersecurity training programs are essential for informing staff about the dangers of phishing emails, social engineering, and other frequent attack vectors. Regular awareness efforts can help organizations build a security-conscious culture, lowering the likelihood of successful assaults.

Data Backup and Recovery

To limit the impact of ransomware attacks, thorough data backup and recovery protocols must be implemented. Backing up vital data to offline or secure offsite locations on a regular basis might help organizations restore their systems and operations without paying the ransom.

Incident Response and Business Continuity Plans

To ensure a quick and successful response to cyber incidents, organizations should design and test incident response plans and business continuity strategies on a regular basis. Roles, responsibilities, communication methods, and steps for containing and recovering from attacks should all be outlined in these plans.

Collaboration and Information Sharing

Sharing information and working with cybersecurity specialists, peers in the business, and government agencies helps improve overall cyber resilience. Organizations should actively participate in information-sharing networks and keep up to date on new dangers and mitigation techniques.

The Newfoundland and Labrador health care records ransom case is a wake-up call.

HOW COULD RISK MANAGEMENT AND RISK ASSESSMENT HAVE BETTER HELPED NFLD HEALTH IN THIS CASE?

Risk management and risk assessment are critical in minimizing and responding to cyber threats such as the ransomware attack on the health care system in Newfoundland and Labrador. Here are how these practices could have aided NFLD Health in this instance:

Identifying Risks

The process of recognizing potential dangers that an organization may encounter is known as risk management. In this scenario, doing a full cybersecurity risk assessment would have assisted in identifying the risks related to cyberattacks and data breaches. This would have given NFLD Health a better understanding of their systems' possible vulnerabilities and allowed them to apply targeted risk mitigation measures.

Risk Analysis and Evaluation

Risk analysis entails determining the likelihood and magnitude of recognized risks. NFLD Health may have identified the probable repercussions of a ransomware assault on healthcare records by analyzing the potential impact in terms of patient privacy, service disruptions, financial losses, and reputational harm. This review would have aided in prioritizing resource allocation to address the most critical concerns.

Risk Mitigation Strategies

Effective risk management entails creating and implementing risk-mitigation methods. In the context of cybersecurity, this would entail putting in place strong security measures like firewalls, intrusion detection systems, data encryption, and regular software updates.

NFLD Health might have better safeguarded its systems and lowered the possibility and impact of a successful attack if it had implemented a proactive risk mitigation plan.

Incident Response Planning

To effectively handle and recover from potential cyber incidents, risk management should include the development of an incident response strategy. In the event of a ransomware attack, this strategy would specify the measures to be taken, including communication channels, data recovery methods, and coordination with law enforcement agencies. With a well-defined incident response plan, NFLD Health might have responded quickly and minimized the damage caused by the attack.

Regular Risk Monitoring and Review

Risk management is a continuing activity that necessitates regular risk monitoring and assessment. NFLD Health could have discovered potential vulnerabilities and emerging threats more effectively if it had implemented continuous monitoring methods and conducted periodic risk assessments. This would have enabled them to modify their risk mitigation methods and strengthen their overall cybersecurity posture.

Employee Training and Awareness

Employees should be educated and trained on cybersecurity best practices as part of risk management. NFLD Health should have enabled its personnel to recognize and report potential threats by boosting awareness about phishing attempts, social engineering techniques, and the significance of secure passwords. Employees who were better informed would have been better able to spot and respond to questionable activity, thereby averting the first intrusion.

By implementing a complete risk management and risk assessment framework, NFLD Health would have been able to identify vulnerabilities, assess potential hazards, build targeted risk mitigation techniques, and create a robust incident response plan. These preventative actions would have placed them in a better position to prevent or lessen the impact of the ransomware assault on their healthcare records.

INFORMATION SECURITY RISK MANAGEMENT (CYBERSECURITY)

In today's interconnected and digitized world, organizations of all sizes and industries must safeguard their information assets and manage cybersecurity threats. The practice of detecting, assessing, and reducing risks to protect the confidentiality, integrity, and availability of sensitive information and essential systems is known as information security risk management.

Organizations face a plethora of cybersecurity dangers as technology continues to grow at a rapid pace, including data breaches, malicious attacks, insider threats, and system vulnerabilities. These risks can result in considerable financial losses, reputational harm, regulatory noncompliance, and operational interruption. As a result, organizations must take a proactive and comprehensive strategy to control information security risks.

Information Security Risk Management is a systematic approach that includes several critical components:

RISK ASSESSMENT

- Identify and assess potential threats and weaknesses in information assets and systems.
- Evaluate the likelihood and consequences of cybersecurity events.
- Examine the present security mechanisms and their efficacy in risk mitigation.

RISK TREATMENT

- Based on the assessment findings, create a risk treatment strategy.
- To decrease risks to a tolerable level, implement suitable security controls and safeguards.
- Prioritize and effectively allocate resources to address the most critical threats.

INCIDENT RESPONSE

- Create an incident response plan to handle and minimize cybersecurity incidents.
- Define the roles and duties, as well as the methods for detecting, responding to, and recovering from security breaches.
- Test and update the incident response strategy on a regular basis to guarantee its efficacy.

SECURITY AWARENESS AND TRAINING

- Employees and stakeholders should be educated about information security threats and best practices.
- Develop a security awareness and vigilance culture throughout the organization.
- Provide cybersecurity training on issues such as phishing awareness, password hygiene, and secure browsing.

CONTINUOUS MONITORING AND IMPROVEMENT

- Implement systems and methods for real-time monitoring and detection of security incidents.
- Review and update security controls on a regular basis to handle evolving threats and vulnerabilities.
- Audit and review the efficiency of the information security program on a regular basis.

COMPLIANCE AND GOVERNANCE

- Ensure that all applicable laws, regulations, and industry standards are followed.

- Create strong governance mechanisms to monitor and manage information security risks.

- Engage stakeholders and build organizational accountability for information security.

- Collaboration and coordination across multiple departments and stakeholders within an organization are required for effective information security risk management. It is not exclusively the duty of the IT department, but also includes management, legal, human resources, and other essential departments.

Furthermore, keeping up with changing cybersecurity trends, threat landscapes, and legislative changes is critical for maintaining a solid information security posture. To improve their risk management efforts, organizations should actively participate in information-sharing programs, attend cybersecurity events, and adopt industry best practices.

Organizations may reduce the risk and impact of cybersecurity incidents, protect sensitive information, and preserve stakeholder trust by taking a proactive and comprehensive approach to Information Security Risk Management. As technology advances, effective cybersecurity risk management will remain a crucial component of any organization's overall risk management approach.

CHAPTER 5

Finance and Risk

FINANCE is essential to every organization, and it is vulnerable to several hazards that might jeopardize its stability, profitability, and long-term existence. Effective risk management and risk assessment are critical in finance to protect assets, maintain regulatory compliance, and make sound financial decisions. This section provides an overview of Finance Risk Management and Risk Assessment, covering essential concepts and aspects.

Market risk, credit risk, liquidity risk, operational risk, and legal and regulatory risk are all examples of potential hazards that fall under the category of financial risks.

- Market risk refers to financial market movements such as interest rates, currency rates, and commodity prices, which can have an influence on investment portfolios and financial instruments.

- Credit risk refers to the chance of borrowers or counterparties defaulting or failing to pay, exposing lenders to potential losses.

- The capacity to acquire adequate funds to meet financial obligations as they become due is referred to as liquidity risk.

- Internal procedures, systems, people, and external events that might disrupt financial operations are all examples of operational risk.

- Legal and regulatory risk is associated with noncompliance with laws, rules, and industry standards, which can result in financial penalties or reputational harm.

Effective finance risk management assists organizations in identifying, assessing, and mitigating possible threats to financial performance. It lets firms design risk reduction plans, preserve assets, and assure regulatory compliance. Finance risk management also helps to improve decision-making processes in capital allocation and investment strategies by optimizing risk-reward trade-offs.

RISK ASSESSMENT IN FINANCE

Risk assessment entails assessing the likelihood and potential impact of identified risks in order to identify their importance and prioritize risk mitigation activities, to analyze risks and forecast prospective losses, risk assessment in finance often uses quantitative techniques such as statistical models, stress testing, and scenario analysis. Organizations can use risk assessment to understand the potential effects of various hazards and make informed decisions about risk management techniques.

RISK MITIGATION STRATEGIES IN FINANCE

Diversification of investments, hedging, insurance, and the establishment of rigorous internal controls and risk management frameworks are all examples of risk reduction measures in finance. In order to limit the impact of credit risk, financial institutions may use credit risk management tools such as credit scoring algorithms, collateral requirements, and credit derivatives. Maintaining adequate cash reserves, arranging lines of credit, and devising contingency plans to overcome unanticipated liquidity shortfalls are all part of effective liquidity risk management.

REGULATORY CONSIDERATIONS

Finance risk management is significantly affected by regulatory frameworks and industry-specific compliance requirements. Organizations must ensure regulatory conformity and execute risk management practices that are consistent with regulatory rules, such as Basel III for banks or International Financial Reporting Standards (IFRS) for financial reporting.

EMERGING TRENDS IN FINANCE RISK MANAGEMENT

Risk management practices must adapt to growing trends and problems in the finance business, which is continually evolving. Artificial intelligence, machine learning, and blockchain technology are revolutionizing risk management procedures by providing real-time monitoring, automated risk assessments, and increased fraud detection. With a greater emphasis on sustainable investing and assessing environmental and social risks in investment portfolios, environmental, social, and governance (ESG) factors are gaining significance in finance risk management. Finance Risk Management and Risk Assessment necessitate an in-depth knowledge of financial concepts, quantitative analysis tools, regulatory frameworks, and industry best practices. Professionals can contribute to the financial stability and success of organizations while limiting potential risks by establishing competence in this area.

MARKET RISK

Market risk is the possibility of financial loss as a result of adverse changes in market pricing or conditions. As it incorporates uncertainties and swings in the larger economic and financial environment, it is a crucial component of overall risk for firms and investors. Individuals and organizations must understand and successfully manage market risk in order to protect their assets, investments, and financial stability.

MARKET RISK CAN BE CAUSED BY A VARIETY OF CAUSES, INCLUDING:

1. *Equity Market Risk*

   This risk is associated with investments in stocks or equity securities. It results from stock price changes caused by factors such as economic conditions, industry trends, company performance, and investor mood. Recessions, political unrest, and industry disruptions can all have a big impact on equity prices.

2. *Interest Rate Risk*

   The risk of losing money owing to changes in interest rates is referred to as interest rate risk. It has an impact on both individuals and businesses who have interest-bearing instruments such as loans, bonds, or savings accounts. When interest rates rise, the value of existing fixed-rate investments falls, and borrowing costs rise, affecting profitability and investment returns.

3. *Currency Exchange Risk*

   Currency exchange risk arises when people or organizations own foreign currency assets or conduct transactions in foreign currency. When changing currencies, fluctuations in exchange rates might result in gains or losses. Businesses engaged in international commerce or investments are especially vulnerable to currency exchange risk.

4. *Commodity Price Risk*

   The exposure to price swings in commodities such as oil, gas, metals, or agricultural items is referred to as commodity price risk. Energy, mining, and agriculture all face inherent risks due to changes in supply and demand dynamics, geopolitical variables, weather patterns, and global market trends.

5.   *Credit Risk*

Credit risk is the possibility of financial loss as a result of borrowers' or counterparties' inability to meet their financial obligations. Market conditions, economic downturns, and changes in creditworthiness can all have an impact on borrowers' capacity to repay loans or meet contractual obligations. This risk is especially important for financial institutions and debt investors.

Market risk management requires a variety of strategies and techniques, including:

1.   *Diversification*

Investing across asset classes, industries, or geographical regions helps to decrease exposure to specific market risks. Diversification enables prospective gains in one area to compensate for losses in another.

2.   *Hedging*

Hedging entails holding offsetting positions to reduce the impact of negative market moves. To hedge against specific risks, techniques such as derivatives, futures contracts, options, and currency hedging can be employed.

3.   *Risk Assessment and Monitoring*

Assessing and monitoring market circumstances on a regular basis, including economic statistics, industry developments, and geopolitical considerations, aids in identifying potential dangers. Portfolio performance monitoring and the use of risk management tools and models can provide insights into exposure and inform decision-making.

4.   *Scenario Analysis and Stress Testing*

Scenario analysis and stress testing assist in determining the potential impact of adverse market conditions on investments or portfolios. Individuals and organizations can assess their resilience and make educated risk management decisions by simulating severe circumstances.

5.   *Risk Mitigation Strategies*

Putting risk mitigation methods in place entails taking proactive steps to decrease market risk exposure. This could entail altering investment allocations, implementing risk- management approaches, or actively managing positions based on market conditions.

Individuals and organizations can protect their investments, improve financial performance, and make informed decisions in volatile and uncertain market settings by properly managing market risk.

CREDIT RISK

Credit risk is an important facet of risk management, especially in the financial sector. It refers to the possible loss a lender or investor may face if a borrower or counterparty fails to meet their financial obligations. Credit risk originates from the chance of borrowers defaulting or failing to pay, as well as changes in their creditworthiness over time.

Understanding and managing credit risk is critical for financial institutions such as banks, credit card firms, and lending institutions, as well as for investors and individuals that offer credit to counterparties. Organizations can minimize possible losses and preserve a healthy financial position by appropriately assessing and minimizing credit risk.

KEY CREDIT RISK COMPONENTS

Default Risk

This is the likelihood that a borrower or counterparty may fail to meet their contractual commitments, such as loan repayment or interest payments. The borrower's financial health, credit history, industry conditions, and macroeconomic factors can all influence default risk.

Creditworthiness Assessment

Assessing borrowers' creditworthiness is a vital stage in credit risk management. It entails assessing their ability and willingness to repay loans by examining their financial documents, credit scores, payment history, and other pertinent indicators. Credit rating agencies are important in evaluating and assigning credit ratings to entities, which indicate their creditworthiness.

Credit Exposure

This refers to the possible financial loss incurred by an institution if a borrower defaults. The quantity of the loan or investment, as well as the terms and circumstances of the credit arrangement, determine credit exposure. Credit exposure must be monitored and controlled in order to limit possible losses and maintain a balanced credit portfolio.

Concentration Risk

Concentration risk occurs when a major amount of a credit institution's portfolio is exposed to a single industry, geographic region, or individual counterparty. Overexposure to a single sector or entity makes the institution more vulnerable to bad developments in that industry. Diversification and risk limitations are utilized to successfully manage concentration risk.

Credit Risk Mitigation

Financial organizations use a variety of measures to reduce credit risk. Collateral requirements, loan covenants, credit insurance, credit derivatives, and risk transfer via securitization are examples of these. Credit risk reduction measures are an effective attempt to limit possible losses and protect the institution's capital.

Credit Monitoring and Management

Credit risk management is a continual activity that necessitates close monitoring of borrowers and counterparties. Credit quality is routinely assessed, financial conditions are reviewed, and changes in borrowers' creditworthiness are tracked. Proactive risk management steps, such as loan restructuring or setting aside provisions for future losses, are enabled by timely recognition of deteriorating credit circumstances.

Regulatory Compliance

Financial institutions are subject to credit risk management legislation and norms. Minimum capital requirements, stress testing, and reporting standards are imposed by regulatory agencies to ensure institutions have appropriate buffers to absorb potential credit losses and maintain financial stability.

Effective credit risk management entails a combination of stringent credit evaluation practices, sensible lending policies, portfolio diversification, and proactive monitoring and management. Organizations can improve their ability to identify, analyze, and mitigate potential credit-related losses by implementing comprehensive credit risk procedures, resulting in more sound and sustainable financial operations.

LIQUIDITY RISK

Liquidity risk is a critical facet of risk management that organizations, especially financial institutions, must understand and efficiently manage. It refers to the possibility that an organization may struggle to satisfy its short-term financial obligations due to a lack of liquid assets or the inability to quickly convert assets into cash without incurring a considerable loss.

Liquidity in finance refers to the ease with which an item can be purchased or sold in the market without producing major price swings. Liquidity risk emerges when an organization's short-term liabilities exceed its ability to turn assets into cash to satisfy those obligations.

Adequate liquidity is critical for an organization's day-to-day operations. It ensures that its payment commitments to suppliers, employees, and other stakeholders are met on schedule. Inadequate liquidity can disrupt operations, harm relationships, and even lead to corporate failure.

Liquidity risk can have serious consequences for an organization's financial stability. If a company is unable to satisfy its short-term obligations, it may be obliged to sell assets at unfavorable prices or borrow at higher interest rates, eroding profitability and weakening the balance sheet.

Regulatory Compliance

To safeguard banks' ability to endure market stress and sustain stability, financial authorities frequently implement specific liquidity requirements. Compliance with these standards is critical for avoiding fines, preserving the organization's reputation, and establishing investor and depositor trust.

Market Perception and Investor Confidence

An organization's liquidity profile affects its reputation and perception of its financial health. Investors, creditors, and other stakeholders regularly monitor liquidity risk indicators to determine an organization's capacity to meet its obligations. A well- managed liquidity pool may create confidence, attract investment, and boost an organization's overall reputation.

Organizations use a variety of tactics and practices to effectively control liquidity risk.

Liquidity Risk Assessment

Organizations should analyze and quantify their liquidity risk exposure on a regular basis. This includes analyzing asset and liability maturity profiles, stress testing liquidity positions under unfavorable scenarios, and identifying potential sources of funding deficits.

Contingency Planning

It is critical to develop contingency plans and provide access to emergency liquidity sources. To overcome potential liquidity interruptions, organizations should find alternate funding sources, create lines of credit with banks, and keep a diverse pool of liquid assets.

Cash Flow Management

Maintaining enough liquidity requires accurate cash flow forecasts and management. To optimize liquidity levels, organizations should regularly monitor cash inputs and outflows, align their cash conversion cycles, and execute efficient cash management practices.

Funding and Capital Structure

Short-term and long-term funding sources must be balanced in organizations. A well- diversified finance and capital structure decreases reliance on short-term borrowing and improves market stability.

Liquidity Stress Testing

Regular liquidity stress tests aid in the identification of vulnerabilities and the assessment of the impact of bad scenarios on liquidity levels. To evaluate the organization's resilience and identify appropriate risk mitigation strategies, these tests encompass modeling diverse market situations, customer behavior, and finance disruptions.

Regulatory Compliance

Companies must stay up to date on current liquidity legislation and ensure compliance with relevant liquidity risk management guidelines and frameworks. This includes maintaining adequate liquidity ratios, meeting reporting obligations, and putting in place internal controls and monitoring measures.

Organizations can improve their financial resilience, operational continuity, and stakeholder confidence by recognizing and effectively managing liquidity risk. A comprehensive strategy for liquidity risk management is critical for navigating volatile market situations and preserving an organization's long-term sustainability.

CHAPTER 6

Operations and Risk

OPERATIONAL RISK MANAGEMENT

Few events can compete with the scale and intricacy of the Olympic Games. The 2012 Summer Olympics in London, United Kingdom, were a shining example of effective operational risk management. This case study will look at the important areas of operational risk management used throughout the event, emphasizing the methods, challenges, and consequences of risk management in such a high-profile multinational meeting.

The 2012 Summer Olympics in London aspired to bring together competitors from all over the world, display extraordinary sporting accomplishments, and provide millions of fans with an unforgettable experience. However, holding an event of this size has operational risks that must be identified, assessed, and managed efficiently in order to ensure smooth operations and a safe atmosphere for all participants.

The London Organizing Committee of the Olympic and Paralympics Games (LOCOG) undertook a thorough risk assessment. They considered a wide range of potential dangers, such as security threats, transportation disruptions, technology failures, natural disasters, and public health problems. The committee might prioritize its efforts and distribute resources accordingly by estimating the likelihood and impact of these threats.

To address identified hazards, LOCOG used a variety of risk mitigation methods. As an example:

- Security: Local law enforcement agencies, intelligence services, and international allies collaborated to create a robust security strategy. Security guards, surveillance systems, and comprehensive background checks were among the measures implemented.

- Transportation: LOCOG collaborated with transportation authorities to create efficient mobility plans that ensured the safe movement of athletes, officials, and spectators. To reduce road congestion hazards, additional measures such as special Olympic lanes and improved public transit services were introduced.

- Technology: The deployment of modern technological systems, such as result management, scoring, and ticketing systems, was meticulously designed and tested in order to reduce the chance of technical failures and assure smooth operations.

Contingency Planning

LOCOG recognized the significance of planning for the unexpected. They devised contingency plans to cover unexpected disruptions such as inclement weather, power outages, or transportation delays. They were able to respond quickly and minimize the impact of unanticipated events because they had backup systems in place.

Stakeholder Communication

Managing operational hazards during the Olympics required effective communication. LOCOG created open channels of communication with important stakeholders including athletes, sponsors, volunteers, and members of the general public. Regular updates, public announcements, and the dissemination of correct information aided in managing expectations, addressing concerns, and ensuring a coordinated reaction in the event of an emergency.

RESULTS AND LESSONS LEARNED

The London Summer Olympics of 2012 successfully controlled operational risks while leaving a legacy. Among the significant outcomes and lessons learned are:

- Security and safety: The event ended without any serious security incidents, confirming the efficacy of the security measures put in place. Throughout the Games, there was a strong commitment to preserving a safe and secure environment.

- Seamless Operations: Despite the event's size and complexity, operations operated efficiently, with few disruptions for participants, officials, and spectators. This result demonstrated the significance of precise planning, sturdy infrastructure, and effective stakeholder cooperation.

- Collaboration and Partnerships: Successful operational risk management needed close collaboration among numerous institutions, including government agencies, commercial sector partners, and international organizations. The event demonstrated the importance of forming strong partnerships and harnessing the expertise of varied stakeholders.

- Risk Legacy: The lessons learned during the London Olympics in 2012 have had a long-term impact on the following Olympic Games and other mega-events around the world. The event's risk management practices have established norms for future host cities, giving significant insights and best practices.

The London Summer Olympics in 2012 served as an outstanding case study in operational risk management. The London Organizing Committee of the Olympic and Paralympics Games successfully managed the operational risks associated with staging a mega-event of this scale by thorough risk identification, effective mitigation measures, comprehensive contingency planning, and stakeholder communication. The consequences and lessons learned from the event continue to affect risk management practices in future events, establishing a legacy in the field of operational risk management.

CHAPTER 7

The Three Lines of Defence Model

THE Three Lines of Defence Model is comprised of different fronts and functions in an organization with different roles. All three lines of defence exist in some form in every organization, regardless of the size or complexity of business operations. Compliance risk management practices are normally strongest when there are three separate and clearly identified Lines of Defence in a model, regardless of how the these are implemented. The Board of Directors and Senior Management must clearly communicate the expectation that information be shared and activities coordinated among each of the three lines that cumulatively are responsible for managing the organization's regulatory and compliance risks through effective application of compliance controls.

Three Lines of Defence

Due to the growing complexity of operations and increased focus of regulatory authorities on AML/KYC compliance culture, the role of Compliance Function has moved far ahead from the conventional approach and now considered as an important and critical function that aims to add positive value in increasing the overall efficiency and effectiveness of Compliance Programme.

Organizations are free to choose any Governance structure to ensure effective compliance risk management, however, the organizations are strongly encouraged to implement an entity wide "Three Lines of Defence (TLOD) model" of Regulatory Compliance.

An outline of the TLOD model is as follows:

- The line departments/managers/staff serve as the First Line of Defence and are primarily responsible for managing compliance risk that are "inherent" in day-to-day activities, processes, and systems for which they are accountable.

- The compliance function, being the Second Line of Defence, is responsible for assisting line managers/departments in designing and implementing adequate controls to manage risks of non-compliance. The CF is also responsible to closely coordinate with other risk management functions of the bank to monitor the adequacy and efficacy of compliance risk controls.

- Internal audit, being the third line of defence, is performed to ensure that compliance controls are designed and operating effectively, to avoid the risks of regulatory non-compliances

Three Lines of Defence

The Three Lines of Defence model is distinguished among three functions or lines that are involved in the effective management of Compliance risks. They are:

- Functions that own and manage risks.
- Functions that oversee risks.
- Functions that provide independent assurance.

First Line of Defence:

As the first line of defence, operational managers own and manage the risks. They also are responsible for implementing corrective actions to address process and control deficiencies. Operational management is responsible for maintaining effective internal controls and for executing risk and control procedures on a day-to-day basis.

Operational management identifies, assesses, controls, and mitigates the regulatory compliance risks, guiding the development and implementation of internal policies and procedures and ensuring that activities are consistent with goals and objectives.

The mid-level managers design and implement detailed procedures that serve as internal controls and supervise execution through their employees. Operational management naturally serves as the first line of defence because controls are designed into systems and processes under their guidance of operational management. There should be adequate managerial and supervisory controls in place to ensure compliance and to highlight control breakdown, inadequate processes, and unexpected events.

Second Line of Defence

The management of an organization establishes a Second Line of Defence, such as risk management and compliance functions, to help build and monitor the activities and controls of the first line of defence. Their specific functions will vary according to organization and industry, but typical functions in this second line of defence include:

- A risk management function (and/or committee) that facilitates and monitors the implementation of effective risk management practices by operational management and assists those defining target risk exposure and reporting adequate risk-related information throughout the organization.

- A compliance function to monitor various specific risks such as noncompliance with applicable laws and regulations. In this capacity, the separate function reports directly to senior management, and in some business sectors, directly to the governing body. Multiple compliance functions often exist in a single organization, with responsibility for specific types of compliance monitoring, such as health and safety, supply chain, environmental, or quality monitoring.

- A controllership function that monitors financial risks and financial reporting issues. Management establishes these functions to ensure the first line of defence is properly designed, in place, and operating as intended. Each of these functions has some degree of independence from the first line of defence, but they are by nature management functions. As management functions, they may intervene directly in modifying and developing the internal control and risk systems. Therefore, the second line of defence serves a vital purpose but cannot offer truly independent analyses to governing bodies regarding risk management and internal controls.

The responsibilities of these functions vary on their specific nature, but can include:

- Supporting management policies, defining roles and responsibilities, and setting goals for implementation.
- Identifying known and emerging regulatory requirements, and issues.
- Providing compliance risk management frameworks.
- Identifying shifts in the organization's compliance risk appetite.
- Facilitating and monitoring implementation of effective compliance risk management practices by compliance department.
- Assisting management in developing compliance processes and controls to manage compliance risks and breaches.
- Providing training on key and major compliance requirements and risk management processes.
- Monitoring the adequacy and effectiveness of internal control, accuracy and completeness of reporting, compliance with laws and regulations, and timely remediation of deficiencies.

Third Line of Defence

The third line of defence includes the internal audit that is performed to ensure that compliance controls are designed and operating effectively, to avoid the risks of regulatory non-compliances. An external audit is also performed by independently third party to check whether the financial statements of the organization are prepared in accordance with applicable financial reporting framework, considering the related regulatory and compliance requirements.

Internal Audit

Internal auditors provide the governing body and senior management with comprehensive assurance based on the highest level of independence and objectivity within the organization. This high level of independence is not available in the second line of defence.

Internal audit provides assurance on the effectiveness of governance, risk management, and internal controls, including the manner in which the first and second lines of defence achieve risk management and control objectives.

The scope of this assurance, which is reported to senior management and to the governing body, usually covers:

- A broad range of objectives, including efficiency and effectiveness of operations; safeguarding of assets; reliability and integrity of reporting processes; and compliance with laws, regulations, policies, procedures, and contracts.

- All elements of the risk management and internal control framework, which includes internal control environment; all elements of an organization's risk management framework (i.e., risk identification, risk assessment, and response); information and communication; and monitoring.

- The overall entity, divisions, subsidiaries, operating units, and functions – including business processes, such as sales, production, marketing, safety, customer functions, and operations – as well as supporting functions (e.g., revenue and expenditure accounting, human resources, purchasing, payroll, budgeting, infrastructure and asset management, inventory, and information technology).

Establishing a professional internal audit activity should be a governance requirement for all organizations. This is not only important for larger and medium-sized organizations but also may be equally important for smaller entities, as they may face equally complex environments with a less formal, robust organizational structure to ensure the effectiveness of its governance and risk management processes.

The internal audit actively contributes to effective organizational governance providing certain conditions fostering its independence and professionalism are met. Best practice is to establish and maintain an independent, adequately, and competently staffed internal audit function, which includes:

- Acting in accordance with recognized international standards for the practice of internal auditing.
- Reporting to a sufficiently high level in the organization to be able to perform its duties independently.
- Having an active and effective reporting line to the governing body.

In exceptional situations in small organizations, certain lines of defence may be combined. For example, there may be instances where the internal audit function has been requested to establish and/or manage the organization's overall compliance risk management or compliance activities. In these situations, internal audit should communicate clearly to the governing body and senior management regarding the impact of the combination. If dual responsibilities are assigned to a single person or department, it would be appropriate to consider separating the responsibility for these functions later to establish the three lines clearly.

External Auditors

External auditors, regulators, and other external bodies reside outside the organization's structure, but they can have an important role in the organization's overall governance and control structure.

This is particularly the case in regulated industries, such as financial services or insurance. Regulators sometimes set requirements intended to strengthen the controls in an organization and on other occasions perform an independent and objective function to assess the whole or some part of the first, second, or third line of defence with regard to those requirements. When coordinated effectively, external auditors, regulators, and other groups outside the organization can be considered as additional lines of defence, providing assurance to the organization's shareholders, including the governing body and senior management.

Given the specific scope and objectives of their missions, however, the risk information gathered is generally less extensive than the scope addressed by an organization's internal three lines of defence.

THREE LINES OF DEFENSE FRAMEWORK IN THE CONTEXT OF THE 2012 LONDON OLYMPICS

First Line of Defense: Operational Management

The operational management responsibility for the day-to-day activity and risk management within the Olympic organizing committee is the first line of defense. This line is responsible for identifying and managing risks related to the Games' different features, including as venue operations, transportation, security, and participant safety. The organizing committee's operational teams utilized risk management practices such as creating complete risk registers, conducting risk assessments, and devising mitigation plans for identified hazards. The first line of defense intended to prevent and minimize hazards at their source by taking a proactive approach to risk management.

Second Line of Defense: Risk Management And Compliance

The risk management and compliance departments provided independent oversight and support to the operational teams as the second line of defense. This line includes dedicated risk management professionals, compliance officers, and internal auditors in the context of the London Olympics. Their responsibility was to ensure that risk management processes were executed successfully, that applicable legislation and standards were followed, and that measures to limit risks were in place. The second line of defense was also critical in monitoring the effectiveness of risk reduction strategies and making suggestions for improvement.

Third Line of Defense: Internal Audit

The internal audit role served as the third line of defense, providing independent assurance and evaluation of the effectiveness of risk management and governance systems. Internal auditors conducted frequent audits and evaluations to assess the adequacy and efficiency of the organizing committee's risk management practices. They verified the implementation of risk-mitigation strategies, assessed policy and procedure compliance, and suggested opportunities for improvement. The internal audit role helps to improve openness and accountability by providing an impartial perspective on the whole risk management system.

Application to the London Olympics

The Three Lines of Defense structure was used to provide effective governance and risk management practices during the preparation and execution of the 2012 Summer Olympics in London. The operational management teams, representing the first line of defense, collaborated closely with numerous stakeholders to identify and manage risks connected with various parts of the Games. They implemented risk management systems, created contingency plans, and ensured that venues and facilities ran well.

The second line of defense, comprised of risk management and compliance professionals, provided expertise in risk detection, analysis, and mitigation to the operating teams. They conducted independent assessments, examined risk registries, and ensured that relevant legislation and standards were followed. Their participation aided in the strengthening of the risk management framework and the promotion of a risk-aware culture throughout the organization.

The internal audit function, as the third line of defense, was crucial in providing objective assurance and evaluation of the risk management practices implemented by the organizing committee. They evaluated the efficiency of risk-mitigation strategies, examined control mechanisms, and highlighted areas for improvement. Their findings and recommendations aided in improving overall governance and risk management.

CHAPTER 8

Insider Risk and Reputational Risk

PEOPLE in any organization play a critical role in shaping its reputation. Employees, executives, stakeholders, and even consumers can all have a substantial impact on an organization's reputation. As a result, managing reputational risk entails identifying and successfully minimizing possible hazards linked with persons. In this section, we will look at the relationship between people in an organization and reputational risk, as well as techniques for efficiently managing this risk.

Employees are the backbone of every firm and have the ability to improve or harm its reputation. Employee actions or behavior, both inside and outside the office, can have a substantial impact on public impression. Unethical behavior, discriminatory behaviors, social media posts, or any action that opposes the organization's values and ethical standards are all prohibited. Fostering a healthy workplace culture, providing ethics training, and enforcing policies and procedures that fit with the intended reputation are all critical.

Executives' and top-level management's actions and behavior have a direct impact on an organization's reputation. Executive scandals or controversies can cause severe reputational harm. Leaders must operate with integrity, honesty, and responsibility, establishing a good example for the rest of the business. Creating a robust ethical framework and creating a compliance culture is critical in managing the reputational risk connected with CEOs.

Stakeholder relationships, such as those with investors, suppliers, and business partners, can have an impact on an organization's reputation. Misconduct or unethical activity on the part of these parties might reflect negatively on the organization. Due diligence and setting clear expectations through contracts and agreements can assist reduce the reputational risk connected with stakeholders and business partners. Regular communication and the development of strong relationships founded on trust and mutual respect are also essential.

Customers' and consumers' experiences and opinions can have a substantial impact on an organization's reputation. Negative reviews, complaints, or product/service failures can all have a negative impact on public impression. Organizations must prioritize customer happiness, provide high-quality products or services, and respond to any problems or difficulties as soon as possible. Developing a strong customer-centric approach and actively engaging with customers can aid in the management of reputational risks linked with this stakeholder group.

No organization is immune to reputational crises, regardless of the precautions adopted. To limit the impact of negative events on reputation, effective crisis management and, communication methods are required. This includes communicating in a timely and honest manner, accepting responsibility, and taking corrective actions to restore trust. Organizations should have a solid crisis management plan in place, complete with designated spokespersons and clear methods for dealing with reputational concerns.

Social media and internet platforms have a significant impact on an organization's reputation in the digital era. Negative comments, viral videos, or disinformation can quickly spread and influence public perception. Organizations should actively monitor and manage their online presence, interact with social media users, and respond to any unfavorable or incorrect information as soon as possible. It is critical to establish a positive internet reputation through consistent messages and aggressive participation.

Continuous monitoring and feedback methods are required to manage reputational risk. This means actively listening to stakeholders, conducting surveys, monitoring social media and news outlets, and keeping up with public opinion. Assessing the effectiveness of risk management techniques on a regular basis and making appropriate adjustments based on feedback can assist firms in staying ahead of potential reputational concerns.

Remember that reputation is earned over time and may be easily ruined. Organizations can mitigate reputational risks and improve their overall reputation by recognizing the role of people within their business and executing effective risk management techniques.

Human Resources (HR) strategies are crucial in managing the reputational risk connected with individuals within a business. Human resources departments are in charge of designing and implementing policies, processes, and initiatives that are consistent with the organization's values and encourage positive employee behavior. Here are several HR strategies that might help with good reputation risk management:

Recruitment and Selection

HR should implement rigorous recruitment and selection processes to verify that potential workers share the organization's values and ethical standards. Conducting rigorous background checks, reference checks, and behavioral evaluations to uncover any potential reputational hazards is part of this process. Organizations can reduce the risk of reputational loss by selecting people with integrity and a strong ethical mentality.

Code of Conduct and Ethics Training

HR should create and convey a thorough code of conduct for all workers that include anticipated behaviors and ethical standards. Employees should be educated about the organization's principles, acceptable behavior, and potential reputational hazards through regular ethics training sessions. To reduce the danger of reputational damage caused by employees' online actions, training should include covering the usage of social media and appropriate online behavior.

Performance Management and Employee Feedback

Effective performance management systems can aid in the identification and resolution of any behavioral or performance concerns that may jeopardize an organization's reputation. HR should establish clear performance expectations and evaluate employee performance on a regular basis. Furthermore, providing employees with feedback and grievance channels can assist in addressing concerns before they escalate and potentially affect the organization's brand.

Employee Engagement and Communication

Human resources should cultivate a healthy organizational culture that promotes open communication, transparency, and employee involvement. Employees who are engaged are more inclined to act in ways that benefit the organization's reputation. HR should create avenues for employees to provide comments, suggestions, and concerns, as well as guarantee that their voices are heard and acknowledged.

Diversity and Inclusion

Promoting diversity and inclusiveness inside the organization not only helps the organization maintain a strong reputation but also helps to avoid reputational problems connected with discriminatory or exclusionary behaviors. Human resources should create and implement policies and activities that promote diversity, equity, and inclusion. This involves encouraging equal opportunity, addressing bias, and fostering a courteous and inclusive workplace.

Confidential Reporting and Whistleblower Protection

In order to encourage employees to report any unethical or possibly destructive behavior without fear of punishment, HR should provide confidential reporting systems and whistleblower protection rules. This allows HR to respond to complaints quickly and mitigate the reputational risks associated with wrongdoing or noncompliance.

Crisis Preparedness and Communication

Human resources should work with other departments to create crisis management plans and communication methods. Establishing rules for managing reputational crises, training personnel on crisis response, and appointing spokespersons who can successfully engage with internal and external stakeholders during a crisis are all part of this. HR should also monitor public sentiment and respond to any reputational threats uncovered through social media or other means as soon as possible.

Ongoing Training and Development

HR should provide staff with ongoing training and development opportunities to help them better understand reputational risk and how to manage it. Training in ethical decision-making, dispute resolution, effective communication, and media relations is included. HR can build a culture of risk awareness and responsible behavior by investing in workers' professional development.

HR procedures are critical in managing the reputational risk connected with individuals inside an organization. HR professionals may help establish a healthy work environment, align employee behavior with business values, and reduce reputational risks that may emerge from employee behaviors or misconduct by applying these techniques.

Maintaining a secure and productive work environment requires ensuring that new hires do not pose hazards such as criminal activity, confidentiality breaches, theft, or high turnover/retention rates. These risks can be considerably reduced by implementing excellent hiring and onboarding practices. Consider the following strategies:

Thorough Background Checks

Perform thorough background checks on all potential hires. This includes background checks for criminals, job verification, and reference checks. Background checks can aid in the identification of any red flags or previous concerns that may suggest a possible risk. Check that your background check procedures are in accordance with local laws and regulations.

Reference Checks

Contact the references provided to learn more about the candidate's work ethic, dependability, and professionalism. Inquire about the candidate's trustworthiness, devotion to secrecy, and ability to work well within a team.

Conduct Interviews

During the interview, ask behavioral-based questions to elicit information about the candidate's ethics and integrity. Inquire about their experience with sensitive information and how they would manage ethical quandaries. Examine their communication abilities and ability to collaborate.

Skills and Competency Assessments

Assess the candidate's technical talents and competency for the role using skill-based evaluations and tests. This guarantees that employees have the essential skills to properly carry out their job tasks, lowering the chance of poor performance or ineptitude.

Non-Disclosure Agreements (NDAs)

NDAs should be used to protect confidential information. Require all workers, including new hires, to sign NDAs outlining their roles in protecting sensitive company information. Stress the significance of confidentiality and the repercussions of breaching it.

Clear Policies and Code of Conduct

Create and convey clear policies and a code of conduct outlining anticipated behavior, ethical standards, and repercussions for wrongdoing. Provide this information to new hires during onboarding and verify they understand and acknowledge these policies.

Robust Onboarding and Training

Implement a thorough onboarding program that includes instruction on corporate policies, security standards, and expectations. Provide specific training on data security, confidentiality, and ethical behavior. Reiterate the significance of these themes and their impact on the company.

Ongoing Performance Management

Regularly evaluate staff performance and handle any issues that arise. Provide feedback, coaching, and assistance to employees to ensure they understand and meet performance standards. Recognize and encourage positive behavior while addressing any indications of potential hazards or wrongdoing.

Employee Assistance Programs (EAP)

Provide an EAP to employees as a resource for personal and professional help. Employee assistance programs (EAPs) can help employees manage personal issues, which can lower the chance of potential dangers or unethical actions.

Exit Interviews

Conduct exit interviews when employees willingly depart the organization. Collect comments from them on their experience, reasons for leaving, and any concerns they may have. This data can assist in identifying areas for improvement and proactively addressing potential difficulties.

Organizations can reduce the risks connected with new recruits by employing these techniques, resulting in a safer and trustworthy work environment. Remember that constant awareness and monitoring are required to address any potential problems that may occur over time.

INSIDER RISK (BRIBERY AND CORRUPTION)

Insider risk, particularly bribery, and corruption, is a danger to enterprises and their reputation. Individuals within the corporation may take advantage of their positions of trust for personal benefit, and engage in unethical acts such as accepting bribes, engaging in corrupt activities, or squandering business resources. To effectively manage insider risks associated with bribery and corruption, a comprehensive approach combining preventive measures, detection procedures, and appropriate actions is required. In this section, we will look at the nature of insider hazards related to bribery and corruption, as well as measures for mitigating them.

Insider risk refers to the hazard posed by employees who have access to sensitive information, resources, or decision-making authority within a company. Insiders may be enticed to engage in unlawful behaviors in the context of bribery and corruption, such as accepting bribes in exchange for favorable treatment or abusing their authority to gain personal benefits. These behaviors can result in reputational harm, legal ramifications, financial losses, and a loss of trust among stakeholders.

Developing and promoting a strong ethical culture is critical for mitigating insider threats such as bribery and corruption. Organizations should develop a code of conduct outlining expected behaviors and ethics. This code should be adequately communicated to all staff, with frequent training and reinforcement. Encouraging open communication channels and reporting methods can also aid in identifying and immediately addressing unethical practices.

Implementing strong regulations and procedures is critical for preventing and detecting bribery and corruption. Gifts and entertainment, conflicts of interest, procurement processes, and financial transactions should all be covered by these policies. Policies should be clear, easy to understand, and updated on a regular basis to reflect changes in rules and best practices. Through effective communication and training initiatives, it is critical to ensure that staffs are aware of and follow these regulations.

Thorough due diligence is essential during the recruiting process to reduce the likelihood of insiders participating in bribery and corruption. Background checks, reference checks, and screening procedures can all assist in identifying persons who have a history of unethical activity. Similarly, when establishing connections with vendors and suppliers, firms should adopt due diligence methods to verify they adhere to ethical norms and do not engage in corrupt tactics.

Implementing effective job segregation and internal controls can assist limit the possibility of collusion and fraudulent bribery and corruption activities. Organizations can develop checks and balances by clearly defining roles and responsibilities and ensuring that no single employee has complete control over essential processes. Internal audits and assessments should be performed on a regular basis to detect any control gaps or possible weaknesses.

Establishing efficient whistleblower processes and reporting channels is essential for promoting openness, accountability, and ethical behavior in any business. Whistleblowing is the act of informing the proper parties or authorities about misconduct, unlawful activity, or rule infractions within an organization. In order to expose misconduct and safeguard the interests of stakeholders, employees, and the general public, whistleblowers are essential.

In order to protect organizations from harmful activities like fraud, corruption, and unethical behavior, whistleblowing methods are essential. They give people a way to express their concerns and aid in the investigation and stoppage of misbehavior. The following are some major factors emphasizing the significance of whistleblower mechanisms:

Fraud Detection and Prevention: Whistleblowers frequently have firsthand knowledge of or concrete proof of illegal or dishonest behavior that could otherwise go unnoticed. Organizations can recognize and take care of such situations quickly by offering a secure and anonymous reporting mechanism.

Protection of Stakeholder Interests: The interests of stakeholders, like as employees, clients, shareholders, and the general public, are protected through whistleblowing systems. Organizations can address risks and avoid potential harm to their stakeholders by enticing people to report misbehavior.

Ethical Compliance and Culture: Developing an ethical culture is crucial for an organization's growth and reputation. Whistleblowing procedures support the idea that unethical behavior will not be tolerated, promoting a compliant and honest culture.

Legal and Regulatory Compliance: Organizations are required by law and regulation in many jurisdictions to set up whistleblowing procedures. It is essential to follow these laws in order to avoid fines and reputational harm.

Several essential elements must be present for whistleblowing systems to be effective:

Whistleblowers need to feel confident that their identity will be safeguarded and that their concerns will be handled in the strictest confidence.

- Anonymity: Giving people the opportunity to report incidents anonymously enables them to do so without worrying about facing consequences.

- Accessibility: All stakeholders should have easy access to reporting channels to ensure that people may voice issues in a convenient and user-friendly way.

- Independence: Whistleblowing procedures should permit direct reporting to unbiased and independent parties, such as ethics hotlines, ombudspersons, or designated compliance officers.

- Timeliness and Responsiveness: Businesses must react quickly to reports of whistleblowers, investigate any allegations, and take the necessary measures within a fair amount of time.

- Protection against Retaliation: People who come forward with information in good faith should be shielded from reprisal or other negative consequences. It is essential to establish policies and processes to stop retaliation.

Organizations can offer a variety of reporting options to encourage insider reporting. These channels could consist of:

Reporting Internally
- Concerns can be brought up directly by staff members with their immediate managers, compliance officials, or supervisors.

- The benefit of resolving problems internally through internal reporting channels is that it fosters a culture of trust and accountability.

- Employers must make sure that staff members are aware of the designated personnel or departments in charge of handling whistleblower reports.

Ethics Hotlines

- Employees and stakeholders can submit issues through confidential and anonymous reporting methods known as ethics hotlines.

- Hotlines can be established inside within the company or outsourced to outside service providers who specialize in reporting ethics violations and whistleblowing.

- They offer a private, unbiased venue for reporting that ensures confidentiality and shields users from reprisals.

- To meet a variety of reporting demands, hotlines may provide several language choices and be accessible round-the-clock.

Online Reporting Platforms

- Organizations can create online reporting portals for anyone to use to submit their electronic whistleblower reports.

- These systems might have dedicated email addresses or secure web forms for reporting issues.

- To protect the identity and anonymity of whistleblowers, online reporting platforms should have strong security mechanisms in place.

Ombudsperson

- Some businesses select an ombudsperson, a neutral third party who acts as a trusted conduit for receiving and looking into whistleblower reports.

- The ombudsperson offers a private, secure setting for people to voice their concerns and can provide advice on the best course of action.

External Reporting

- People occasionally prefer to report issues to outside authorities, regulatory groups, or law enforcement organizations.
- To ensure that people are aware of their rights and protections, organizations should provide information and guidance on the pertinent external reporting channels available to them.

Whistleblowing Policies and Procedures

- Organizations should develop detailed policies and procedures for reporting misconduct.
- The procedures for reporting issues, the channels that can be used, and the measures taken to protect whistleblowers from reprisal should all be outlined in these policies.
- All employees and stakeholders should be informed of the whistleblowing policies, so they are aware of their rights and the channels accessible to them.

Awareness and Training

   Organizations must educate staff members about the value of reporting wrongdoing and the many avenues for doing so.

- The organization's commitment to integrity and accountability can be emphasized through training programs that teach staff how to identify and report misconduct.

Remember that the organization's dedication to developing a culture that promotes open communication, protects whistleblowers, and responds quickly to expressed concerns determines the efficacy of whistle blowing processes and reporting channels.

Ongoing Monitoring and Data Analysis

Continuous monitoring of financial transactions, expense reports, and other pertinent data can aid in the detection of patterns or abnormalities that may indicate bribery or corruption. Monitoring efforts can be made more effective by utilizing data analytics and automated monitoring solutions. Internal controls, audits, and risk assessments should be reviewed on a regular basis to identify opportunities for improvement and assure compliance with anti-corruption measures.

Enforcement and Consequences

To deter and resolve cases of bribery and corruption, organizations must build a strong enforcement framework. Individuals found guilty of engaging in such activities face severe disciplinary actions, including firing. Furthermore, companies should work with law enforcement and regulatory agencies to guarantee that persons involved in bribery and corruption face legal penalties.

Organizations can effectively manage insider risks connected to bribery and corruption by using a holistic approach that involves preventive measures, detection procedures, and appropriate remedies. Fostering an ethical culture, enforcing strict standards, doing due diligence, and fostering openness are all critical elements in reducing this risk and safeguarding the organization's reputation and integrity.

CONFIDENTIALITY AGREEMENTS

HR rules, especially confidentiality agreements, are critical in protecting an organization in a variety of ways. Confidentiality agreements are legal instruments that specify the organization's expectations and obligations for the preservation of sensitive information. Here are some examples of how good practices, such as confidentiality agreements, can safeguard the organization:

1. *Protection of Intellectual Property*

    Confidentiality agreements protect the organization's intellectual property, which includes trade secrets, confidential information, R&D, and other important assets. These agreements help prevent employees from disclosing sensitive information with competitors or the general public by explicitly defining what constitutes confidential information and banning its unauthorized disclosure.

2. *Safeguarding Client and Customer Information*

    Many sectors deal with sensitive information about their clients or customers. Confidentiality agreements ensure that staff keeps this information private and secret. This safeguards the firm against legal ramifications such as data breaches, privacy violations, or illegal use or disclosure of personal or sensitive data.

3. *Maintaining Competitive Advantage*

    Companies achieve a competitive advantage by building distinctive processes, strategies, and market insights. Employees are prohibited from disclosing such secret knowledge with competitors under confidentiality agreements, which helps to maintain the organization's competitive advantage and protects it from potential exploitation or imitation.

4. *Preserving Business Relationships*

    Confidentiality agreements can be critical in retaining trust and business partnerships. When organizations collaborate or form alliances, they frequently share sensitive information. These agreements ensure that the information supplied remains confidential, fostering confidence among partners and safeguarding the organization's reputation and relationships.

5. *Preventing Employee Poaching*

   Confidentiality agreements can help protect a business against staff poaching in areas where competent people are in high demand. Non-solicitation clauses in these agreements often prohibit employees from soliciting or recruiting other employees to join competitor firms. Confidentiality agreements assist in organizational stability and continuity by preventing the loss of essential individuals.

6. *Compliance with Legal and Regulatory Requirements*

   Confidentiality agreements can assist a company in meeting legal and regulatory requirements concerning the safeguarding of sensitive information. Healthcare and banking, for example, have stringent regulations governing the privacy and confidentiality of client/patient data. Implementing confidentiality agreements guarantees that these requirements are followed and avoids the danger of legal fines.

7. *Mitigating Risks of Insider Threats*

   Insider threats, such as unauthorized access, data theft, or employee sabotage, can pose serious hazards to enterprises. Confidentiality agreements act as a deterrent by explicitly establishing the expectations and consequences of using or disclosing confidential information improperly. They raise employee understanding of their responsibilities and the potential penalties for breaching confidentiality obligations.

8. *Establishing a Culture of Confidentiality*

   Implementing robust confidentiality agreements and related regulations fosters an organizational culture of confidentiality. Employees learn about the organization's commitment to preserving sensitive information and their role in ensuring confidentiality. This confidentiality culture strengthens the organization's overall security posture.

It is critical to remember that the effectiveness of confidentiality agreements is dependent on proper execution, clear communication, and enforcement. Regular training and education regarding the importance of confidentiality, the penalties for violations, and reporting processes for any violations can help to reinforce the protection given by these agreements. Good HR policies, particularly confidentiality agreements, provide an important layer of security for firms by securing intellectual property, client/customer information, competitive advantage, business relationships, and regulatory compliance. They also assist in reducing the dangers of insider threats and establishing a culture of secrecy within the firm.

Reputational Risk

Several issues can jeopardize your public image and possibly harm your reputation. It is critical to be aware of these dangers and to take preventative measures to mitigate them. Here are some examples of common circumstances that can harm your public image:

1. *Misconduct and Unethical Behavior*

   Misconduct, unethical behavior, or illegal acts can seriously harm your public image. Fraud, corruption, prejudice, and environmental infractions are examples of such issues. Any action that goes against ethical standards and principles can cause public outrage and a loss of trust.

2. *Product or Service Failures*

   It can affect your reputation if your products or services frequently fail to fulfill customer expectations or pose dangers to health, safety, or the environment. Recalls, quality difficulties or a high volume of customer complaints can erode faith in your brand and harm your public image.

3.   *Data Breaches and Privacy Incidents*

Data breaches and privacy issues can have serious ramifications for an organization's reputation in today's digital landscape. Mishandling of consumer data, unauthorized access, or failure to protect sensitive information can result in public outrage, loss of customer trust, and legal ramifications.

4.   *Poor Customer Service*

Inadequate customer service or neglecting to appropriately address consumer problems might affect your public image. Negative customer experiences shared via reviews, social media, or word-of-mouth can have a substantial influence on your reputation, as customer satisfaction is critical in influencing public perception.

5.   *Crisis Mishandling*

How you handle a crisis or emergency scenario can have a significant impact on your public image. Poor crisis management, a slow reaction, or a lack of transparency can exacerbate the issue and undermine trust. During a crisis, effective communication, quick response, and accepting responsibility is critical for minimizing reputational harm.

6.   *Negative Media Coverage and Public Perception*

The media has a large influence on public opinion. Negative media coverage, sensationalism, or false reporting can swiftly sully your reputation. Furthermore, public perception can be influenced by social media discussions, viral material, or online rumors, which can have a negative impact on your reputation.

7. *Social and Environmental Impact*

   Organizations are increasingly being evaluated based on their social and environmental activities. Any activities or practices deemed harmful to societal well-being or the environment might jeopardize a company's reputation. Failure to address environmental issues, labor infractions, or community alienation can result in public outrage and harm your reputation.

8. *Inconsistent Brand Messaging*

   Inconsistencies in brand messages, beliefs, or promises can cause misunderstanding and erode confidence. A gap between what you claim to stand for and your actual conduct can jeopardize your public image. Maintaining a positive reputation requires consistency in conveying your brand values and aligning them with your activities.

   Organizations should prioritize ethical behavior, transparency, open communication, and a customer-centric strategy to mitigate these threats. Establishing effective risk management and crisis management methods, actively monitoring public mood, and responding quickly to any concerns that develop are critical for safeguarding and keeping your public image.

WHAT INDIVIDUALS CAN RISK YOUR PUBLIC IMAGE?

Several persons both inside and outside of an organization can jeopardize its public image. Their activities, behavior, or relationships can have a substantial impact on how the public perceives the company. Here are some people who can jeopardize your reputation:

1. *Employees*

   Employees at all levels of a company can have an impact on the organization's public image. Employee misconduct, unethical behavior, or inappropriate behaviors can harm the organization's reputation. This includes discriminatory activities, harassment, unfavorable social media posts about the organization, and any behavior that goes against the organization's values and ethical standards.

2. *Executives and Leadership*

    Executives and top-level management play a vital role in defining an organization's public image. Executive misconduct or involvement in scandals can have serious consequences for their reputation. This covers incidents of fraud, embezzlement, conflicts of interest, or any other action that is illegal or unethical. Executive actions viewed as lacking in honesty or openness can likewise be detrimental to the organization's reputation.

3. *Spokespersons or Public Representatives*

    Individuals who serve as the organization's spokespersons or public representatives have a tremendous impact on its public image. Their remarks, activities, or contentious associations may attract public notice and influence how the organization is seen. Incorrect or insensitive words, public gaffes, or any action that contradicts the organization's messaging can all harm the organization's reputation.

4. *Influencers or Brand Ambassadors*

    To advertise their products or services, businesses frequently work with influencers or brand ambassadors. If these employees participate in inappropriate behavior, or scandals, or publicly express ideas that are contradictory to the organization's ideals, the organization's public image may suffer. To mitigate such hazards, it is critical to thoroughly screen and monitor the conduct of influencers and brand ambassadors.

5. *Board Members and Directors*

    Board members and directors bear considerable responsibilities for the governance and strategic direction of the business. Their activities, conflicts of interest, and involvement in issues might jeopardize their reputation. Financial impropriety, noncompliance with regulations, or inability to perform their fiduciary duties can all be detrimental to an organization's reputation.

6. *Business Partners and Suppliers*

    Associations with business partners and suppliers can potentially jeopardize one's reputation. If these organizations engage in unethical behavior, environmental problems, or human rights violations, it might reflect negatively on the organization. Due diligence and the establishment of clear expectations through contracts and agreements are critical in controlling such risks.

7. *Customers or Users*

    Customers or users who are dissatisfied with the organization's products or services may damage its reputation through reviews, word-of-mouth, or social media. Responding quickly to customer issues and delivering outstanding customer service is critical in mitigating the reputational risks connected with this group.

    While individuals can be a source of reputational risk, effective risk management measures like as clear regulations, ethical guidelines, training programs, and proactive monitoring can help limit these risks. Building a culture of integrity, accountability, and transparency throughout the organization is critical for mitigating potential public image challenges.

CHAPTER 9

Black Swan Risks and Business Continuity Planning

Bᴸᴀᴄᴋ swan risks are unusual and extremely unpredictable events that have a significant impact and frequently catch people, businesses, or society off guard. The concept of black swan events, coined by Nassim Nicholas Talab, stems from the belief that all swans were white until the discovery of black swans in Australia. Similarly, black swan risks are situations that are thought to be exceedingly uncommon or impossible until they occur.

Black Swan Risks have the following characteristics:

Rarity

Because of their rarity, black swan risks are remarkable events that are difficult to forecast or anticipate. They exist outside of regular expectations and statistical models.

Severe Impact

Black swan occurrences have far-reaching and frequently disastrous consequences for individuals, businesses, and society. Their ramifications can be far-reaching and long-lasting.

Hindsight Bias

Following a black swan event, there is a propensity to feel that it was predicted or that the warning signs were obvious in retrospect. However, because black swan risks are unpredictable, they are difficult to predict in advance.

Lack of Precedence

Black swan hazards frequently have no historical precedent or point of reference. They put existing knowledge and assumptions to the test, making it difficult to foresee or handle them successfully.

EXAMPLES OF BLACK SWAN RISKS INCLUDE

Global Financial Crisis (2008)

The 2008 Global Financial catastrophe (GFC) was a serious global economic catastrophe with far-reaching effects for the global economy. It was precipitated by several events, including the bursting of the housing bubble in the United States, excessive risk- taking by financial institutions, and the growth of sophisticated financial products.

Causes of the Global Financial Crisis

The crisis began with the collapse of the housing market in the United States. Years of loose lending rules and the issuing of subprime mortgages contributed to the formation of a housing bubble. When property values began to fall, homeowners began to fail on their mortgages, resulting in a rapid increase in defaults on mortgage-backed securities.

Mortgages were packaged by financial institutions into complex financial products known as mortgage-backed securities (MBS) and collateralized debt obligations (CDOs). These products were then marketed and exchanged globally among financial institutions. Investors found it difficult to adequately estimate the risks associated with these instruments due to their complexity and lack of transparency.

By substantially investing in mortgage-backed securities and highly leveraged investments, many financial institutions took on excessive risks. They overestimated the dangers involved by assuming that the housing market would continue to increase. When the housing bubble burst, many institutions suffered large losses and liquidity issues.

Financial institutions' risk management strategies were insufficient in analyzing and mitigating the risks associated with mortgage-backed securities. In addition, regulatory organizations failed to adequately oversee and regulate the financial industry, allowing hazardous activities to continue unabated.

The Global Financial Crisis's Aftermath

The 2008 Global Financial Crisis caused a catastrophic economic slump, with recessions and negative growth in economies all across the world. The crisis had a significant influence on several industries, including manufacturing, services, and employment, resulting in widespread job losses and decreased consumer spending.

Several big financial firms were declared bankrupt or required government assistance to avoid collapse. Governments around the world, particularly in the United States and Europe, enacted enormous rescue plans to stabilize the financial system and prevent a total disaster.

Global stock markets saw severe drops, with many indices dropping to historic lows. Investors suffered significant losses, and investor trust in financial markets was seriously undermined.

The crisis caused a lengthy downturn in the housing market, with dropping property values and more foreclosures. Many homeowners ended up with negative equity, owing more on their mortgages than their properties were worth.

Following the Global Financial Crisis, officials implemented regulatory reforms aimed at strengthening the financial system and minimizing the possibility of another crisis. Dodd-Frank Wall Street Reform and Consumer Protection Act in the United States and Basel III internationally designed to strengthen risk management, boost capital requirements, and improve transparency and monitoring.

Lessons Learned and Ongoing Impact

The Global Financial Crisis exposed fundamental vulnerabilities in risk management techniques, regulatory oversight, and the global financial system's interdependence. Among the most important lessons acquired are:

- The requirement for strong risk management methods and an in-depth understanding of complicated financial instruments.

- The significance of good regulation and oversight in preventing excessive risk-taking and ensuring the financial system's stability.

- The significance of financial transaction and reporting openness and accountability.

- Recognizing the global nature of financial markets and the importance of international cooperation in dealing with systemic threats.

The global economy and banking industry are still feeling the effects of the GFC. It has changed investor behavior and heightened scrutiny of financial institutions' risk management strategies, shaping the regulatory landscape.

COVID-19 Pandemic

The COVID-19 pandemic has had a significant impact on the global society, affecting communities, economies, and healthcare systems all around the world. COVID-19 developed in late 2019 as a highly contagious respiratory illness caused by the novel corona virus SARS-CoV-2 and quickly spread across the globe, causing enormous health, social, and economic effects.

Health Effect

Millions of people have been infected by the virus, resulting in a huge number of diseases and fatalities. It has placed a huge strain on healthcare systems, especially those with little resources and infrastructure. COVID-19 has been shown to produce severe respiratory symptoms ranging from moderate to life-threatening. Individuals with pre-existing health issues, as well as the elderly, are especially prone to severe sickness and death. Long-term health impacts of the virus have also been discovered, including respiratory difficulties, organ damage, neurological complications, and chronic symptoms described as "Long COVID."

Social Impact

The epidemic has demanded stringent public health measures such as social isolation, lockdowns, and travel restrictions, which have had an influence on people's daily lives and social contacts. These procedures were designed to limit viral transmission and safeguard vulnerable populations. Closures or restrictions have been imposed on schools, companies, and public spaces, affecting education, employment, and leisure activities. For many people, remote work and virtual learning have become the new standard. Because of variables such as fear of infection, social isolation, and economic instability, the pandemic has created psychological distress, including higher levels of stress, anxiety, and depression.

Economic Impact

The epidemic has caused a huge decline in the worldwide economy. Businesses in a variety of industries encountered closures, curtailed operations, and financial difficulties. Many people have lost their employment or had their income reduced. The availability of products and key supplies was impacted as supply routes were interrupted. Travel, tourist, hospitality, and entertainment industries were particularly heavily hit. To minimize the economic damage, governments enacted fiscal and monetary measures such as stimulus packages, financial aid, and support programs for affected firms and individuals.

Healthcare Systems

The epidemic put an enormous strain on healthcare infrastructure, resulting in a lack of medical supplies, hospital beds, and healthcare workers. Efforts were made to enhance testing capacity quickly, produce vaccinations, and dedicate resources to treating COVID-19 patients. Telemedicine and remote healthcare services have grown in popularity to provide healthcare while reducing the danger of transmission.

Scientific Advances

The pandemic of COVID-19 prompted unprecedented global collaboration among scientists, researchers, and healthcare professionals. This collaboration resulted in faster vaccine development, better diagnostics, and more treatment alternatives. The pandemic underscored the significance of a strong public health infrastructure, surveillance systems, and worldwide collaboration in responding to emerging infectious illnesses.

Societal Changes

The epidemic prompted the broad use of remote work, virtual meetings, and e- commerce, fundamentally altering how people work, interact, and conduct business. Hygiene procedures like as frequent hand washing, mask use, and surface sanitization have become critical preventive measures. COVID-19 also highlighted and worsened existing social inequities, such as gaps in healthcare access, income, and education.

Vaccination Drives

COVID-19 vaccines have been produced and deployed globally, providing hope for curbing the virus's spread. Vaccination initiatives were designed to create herd immunity and safeguard vulnerable people. During the pandemic, vaccine distribution, vaccination reluctance, and equal access to vaccines were major concerns. The COVID-19 pandemic is a sharp reminder of the significance of planning, effective risk management, and global cooperation in dealing with complex health crises. It has hastened innovation, transformed societies, and highlighted the importance of resilient healthcare.

Terrorist Attacks

Terrorism is a huge risk that endangers individuals, communities, and nations all around the world. Understanding and mitigating the risks connected with terrorist attacks is a critical component of risk management. In this section, we will go deeper into the issue of terrorist attacks, exploring their characteristics, consequences, and risk-mitigation techniques.

Terrorist acts are distinguished using violence, intimidation, and terror to achieve ideological, political, or religious goals. Here are some important factors to consider:

Terrorist acts are frequently motivated by a variety of beliefs and reasons, such as political extremism, separatism, religious fundamentalism, or a desire for societal change. Understanding the underlying motivations is critical for analyzing and mitigating the risks posed by various terrorist organizations.

Terrorist attacks can take many different forms, such as bombings, armed assaults, hijackings, and cyber-attacks. Crowded public locations, transportation systems, government institutions, religious sites, and iconic landmarks might all be targets. Terrorists seek to maximize casualties, cause infrastructure damage, and instill widespread fear and panic.

Terrorism can have global as well as local characteristics. While some terrorist organizations operate on a global scale, others are more regional or domestic in nature. When assessing the dangers connected with terrorist attacks, it is critical to consider the geopolitical backdrop, regional dynamics, and historical variables.

Terrorist attacks can have far-reaching and life-changing consequences for individuals, society, and the economy. Here are some significant outcomes:

1. *Loss of Life and Physical Injuries*

    The loss of innocent lives and the physical damage inflicted on victims are the most immediate and terrible consequences of terrorist acts. These attacks can result in considerable human suffering and long-term physical and psychological anguish for survivors.

2. *Economic Disruption*

    Terrorist strikes have the potential to interrupt economic activity and harm essential infrastructure, resulting in significant economic losses. Tourism, transportation, and commerce are especially sensitive to the results of attacks, which can lead to lost investor confidence and long-term economic ramifications.

3.   *Social and Psychological Effects*

Terrorist attacks are designed to instill fear, mistrust, and division among societies. They have the potential to exacerbate societal polarization, discrimination, and stigma. Communities may experience increased fear, distrust, and vulnerability, affecting social cohesion and overall well-being.

Mitigating the Risks of Terrorist Attacks

Risk management measures are critical in managing the dangers posed by terrorist attacks. Here are some important considerations:

1.   *Threat Assessment*

Conduct extensive threat assessments to identify prospective targets, vulnerabilities, and terrorist groups' capabilities. Collaborate with intelligence agencies, law enforcement, and security specialists to acquire accurate information and keep up to date on emerging risks.

2.   *Security Measures*

To safeguard possible targets, establish comprehensive security measures such as improving physical security, installing surveillance technologies, and creating access control protocols. Create emergency response plans and practice drills to ensure that you are prepared and can respond effectively in the event of an attack.

3. *Information and intelligence sharing*

    Create strong procedures for exchanging intelligence and information across key stakeholders, such as government agencies, law enforcement, and international partners. Timely and accurate information exchange can aid in the identification of new hazards and the implementation of preventative measures.

4. *Public Awareness and Vigilance*

    Promote public awareness programs that educate people about the indicators of suspicious activity and encourage them to be vigilant. Encourage residents to report any suspicious behavior to authorities using the "see something, say something" philosophy.

INTERNATIONAL COOPERATION

Terrorism is a worldwide problem that necessitates international cooperation. Encourage international cooperation in counterterrorism activities by sharing best practices, intelligence, and resources. Participate in several activities

While it is hard to completely forecast or prevent black swan events, there are techniques that can assist reducing their impact:

1. *Robust Risk Management:*

    Implement a solid risk management system that considers both known risks and the possibility of black swan events. This includes scenario preparation, stress testing, and reviewing risk mitigation techniques on a regular basis.

2. *Flexibility and Agility:*

    Develop an organizational culture of adaptation and resilience. Encourage adaptability and the ability to respond quickly to unforeseen situations. Maintaining enough reserves, diversifying investments, and having contingency plans in place can all contribute to this.

3. *Redundancy and Reducing Interdependencies:*

    Identify and decrease single points of failure in an organization's important systems, processes, and dependencies. Building redundancy and alternate solutions can assist in mitigating the impact of black swan incidents.

4. *Continuous Learning and Improvement:*

    Encourage a learning mentality and foster information and knowledge sharing within and across businesses. Review and adjust risk management plans on a regular basis depending on new insights and experiences.

5. *Scenario Analysis and Stress Testing:*

    Perform scenario analysis and stress tests to evaluate the resilience of systems, processes, and portfolios in the face of harsh and unexpected events. This can aid in the identification of vulnerabilities and the development of risk mitigation methods.

6. *Insurance and Risk Transfer:*

    To reduce the financial impact of black swan events, consider proper insurance coverage and risk transfer arrangements. This may entail collaborating with insurance companies or investigating alternate risk transfer solutions.

    While measures can aid in the management of black swan risks, total prevention or prediction is rare. To negotiate the uncertain and unpredictable character of black swan events, the emphasis should be on developing resilience, adaptability, and a proactive approach to risk management.

FORCE MAJEURE (COVID; NATURAL DISASTER)

Force majeure events and natural disasters are unforeseeable occurrences that can severely interrupt company operations, initiatives, and contractual commitments. These uncontrollable events can have far-reaching implications and pose significant hazards to enterprises. Understanding force majeure and natural disasters is critical for risk management and devising mitigation methods. This lesson will examine the notion of force majeure, look at real-world examples of natural disasters, and evaluate the consequences for businesses and risk management.

Force majeure refers to unanticipated circumstances that prevent or delay the performance of contractual obligations and are caused by events beyond the party's control. These occurrences are often unforeseen, inescapable, and the result of exogenous circumstances beyond human control. Contracts typically include force majeure clauses to give legal protection and remedies to parties in the case of such situations.

Examples of force majeure events include:

1. *Natural Disasters*

    Natural disasters are catastrophic events caused by natural processes that can inflict widespread destruction, loss of life, and economic disruption. These catastrophes are often beyond human control and, depending on the sort of disaster, can occur immediately or gradually.

    Earthquakes: Seismic events that cause extensive infrastructure damage, creating supply chain interruptions and project delays.

    Hurricanes and Cyclones: Violent storms with tremendous winds and heavy rains that can destroy buildings, infrastructure, and transportation networks.

Floods: are caused by excessive rainfall or river overflow, resulting in extensive inundation, infrastructure damage, and service disruption.

Wildfires: Uncontrolled fires that spread quickly and destroy ecosystems, properties, and infrastructure.

Tsunamis: are large ocean waves caused by seismic activity that can cause catastrophic devastation in coastal communities.

Volcanic eruptions: Volcanic eruptions of molten rock, ash, and gas can disrupt air travel, taint water sources, and harm infrastructure.

2. *Political or Social Unrest*

    Civil wars, revolutions, or societal movements wreak havoc on commercial operations, logistics, and security.

    Imposition of trade embargoes, sanctions, or government interventions that impede normal company operations.

3. *Acts of Terrorism*

    Deliberate acts of violence or damage, such as bombings, hijackings, and cyber-attacks, that can severely disrupt businesses and infrastructure.

IMPLICATIONS FOR BUSINESSES AND RISK MANAGEMENT:

Natural disasters and force majeure events can have serious consequences for organizations and risk management. Among the most important considerations are:

- Operational Disruptions: Supply chain, transportation network, utility, and essential infrastructure disruptions can stymie business operations, resulting in delays, production losses, and revenue consequences.

- Financial Consequences: The costs of rebuilding, repairing, and recovering can put a strain on financial resources. Insurance and financial contingency planning are critical in avoiding financial losses.

- Legal and contractual duties: Force majeure occurrences may cause force majeure clauses in contracts to be activated, offering relief and protection to parties that are unable to fulfill their obligations. Contracts should be reviewed to determine the applicability and ramifications of force majeure clauses.

- Risk Mitigation and Resilience: Effective risk management techniques include recognizing and assessing natural disasters and force majeure occurrences as part of the total risk profile. Organizational resilience can be improved by developing mitigation plans, business continuity strategies, and disaster response practices.

Force majeure and force majeure occurrences are significant forces that can disrupt corporate operations, initiatives, and contractual commitments. Understanding these occurrences and their consequences are critical for good risk management. Organizations can build strategies to limit the impact of force majeure and natural disasters by recognizing potential hazards. This improves their ability to manage and recover from such difficult circumstances.

FORCE MAJEURE AND THE COVID-19 PANDEMIC

The COVID-19 pandemic that developed in 2019 has had a dramatic influence on businesses and individuals around the world, causing disruptions in a variety of industries. In this section, we will look at the use of force majeure in the context of the COVID-19 pandemic, including its ramifications and pertinent examples.

THE COVID-19 PANDEMIC AND FORCE MAJEURE

Because of its unparalleled impact on global health, economy, and supply chains, the COVID-19 pandemic has been designated as a force majeure event in multiple contracts. The outbreak resulted in government-imposed lockdowns, travel restrictions, supply chain disruptions, labor shortages, and business temporary closures, all of which had a severe impact on contractual performance.

Example 1: Travel and Hospitality Industry

Consider the following scenario: A hotel has agreed to host a huge conference. However, due to the COVID-19 pandemic and related travel restrictions, the conference organizers canceled the event. In this situation, the contract's force majeure clause could shield the hotel from liability for non-performance because the pandemic and associated travel restrictions were unforeseeable occurrences that made performance impossible or impractical.

Example 2: Manufacturing and Supply Chain Disruptions

Assume an electronic component manufacturer has a contract with a buyer to provide a certain quantity of products within a certain deadline. However, because of the pandemic, the manufacturer's supply chain was severely disrupted, resulting in a shortage of raw materials and personnel. As a result, the manufacturer may utilize the force majeure clause to justify delivery delays or contract non-performance.

Implications and Challenges

While force majeure can provide relief when contractual commitments become impossible or unreasonable to complete, its application during the COVID-19 pandemic has produced various questions and controversies. Some of the most important consequences and challenges are as follows:

1. *Interpretation of Force Majeure Clauses*

    The terminology used in force majeure clauses, as well as the exact situations covered, can differ from contract to contract. Parties may disagree over whether the epidemic is covered by the clause, resulting in legal problems and interpretations.

2. *Notice and Documentation Requirements*

    Many force majeure provisions require parties to give timely notice and evidence of the occurrence and its impact on contractual performance. Failure to meet these standards may limit or invalidate the use of force majeure.

3. *Mitigation and Optimal Performance*

    Parties who invoke force majeure are frequently obligated to take reasonable steps to reduce the impact of the incident or to investigate other means of performing their obligations. The scope of such activities may also become a source of controversy and potential conflict.

4. *Insurance Protection*

    The availability and scope of insurance coverage for losses caused by force majeure events, like as the COVID-19 pandemic, can differ. To determine the application of coverage, parties may need to analyze their insurance policies and negotiate with insurers.

    Due to its considerable impact on contractual performance, the COVID-19 pandemic has sparked a worldwide wave of force majeure claims. While force majeure can give a legal basis for parties to seek release from their commitments, its use is dependent on the individual circumstances, contract language, and applicable laws. It is critical for parties to carefully evaluate their contracts, assess the impact of the pandemic, and get legal counsel as needed to negotiate the intricacies and potential disputes stemming from force majeure claims linked to the COVID-19 pandemic.

5. *Contractual Implications*

    When a force majeure event happens, it is critical to evaluate the contract provisions to identify the parties' rights and obligations. Contracts may define how to use force majeure, such as giving notice within a specific date or demonstrating that performance has become impossible or commercially unfeasible. Furthermore, force majeure clauses frequently specify the event's repercussions, such as the suspension of obligations, termination rights, or alternative dispute resolution processes.

Mitigating and Managing Force Majeure Risks

To properly handle force majeure risks, the following techniques must be considered:

*   *Contractual Considerations*
    *   Carefully construct force majeure clauses that clearly identify the triggering events as well as the parties' rights and obligations.
    *   Include clauses requiring notice, mitigating attempts, alternative performance choices, and dispute resolution processes.
    *   To address future health crises, consider including "pandemic" or specific diseases in force majeure provisions.

*   *Risk Assessment and Contingency Planning*
    *   Conduct a thorough risk assessment to identify potential force majeure situations that may have an impact on your organization.
    *   Create contingency plans outlining alternate alternatives to meeting contractual commitments in the case of a force majeure incident.

- Establish communication routes and protocols to notify stakeholders and debate potential solutions as soon as possible.

- *Insurance Coverage*
  - Examine insurance plans to determine the extent of coverage for force majeure occurrences such as natural catastrophes and pandemics.
  - Consider purchasing additional coverage for occurrences that are not generally covered by standard insurance.

- *Business Continuity and Resilience*
  - Implement business continuity plans to lessen the impact of force majeure events on operations and to assure a quick recovery.
  - Diversify your suppliers and   make backup plans to avoid supply chain interruptions caused by force majeure occurrences.
  - Maintain a solid crisis management framework, complete with defined roles and duties, communication plans, and decision-making processes.

Events of force majeure can severely impair business operations and contractual commitments. Organizations may negotiate these difficult conditions and reduce the possible impact on their operations and contractual relationships by understanding force majeure provisions, proactively managing risks, and developing suitable contingency plans.

BUSINESS CONTINUITY PLANNING

Business Continuity Planning (BCP) is a proactive strategy for ensuring that an organization's vital operations and delivery of essential products or services can continue in the face of various disruptions or crises. It entails developing and implementing strategies, procedures, and policies to reduce the impact of potential hazards and allow the business to recover swiftly and effectively. We will look at the essential components and actions involved in business continuity planning in this section.

Risk Assessment and Business Impact Analysis

Conducting a complete risk assessment and business impact analysis is the first stage in business continuity planning. This includes assessing potential threats and hazards, such as natural disasters, cyber-attacks, pandemics, or power outages, that could disrupt routine operations. A business impact study also assists in assessing the potential effects of these disruptions on essential processes, resources, and stakeholders. This research lays the groundwork for the development of successful mitigation solutions.

Business Continuity Plan Development

After identifying the risks and potential consequences, the next step is to create a business continuity strategy. This plan outlines the strategies, procedures, and resources needed to keep or restore critical business functions during and after a disruption. Clear roles and duties, communication methods, backup systems, and recovery strategies should all be included in the strategy. Alternative sites, supply chain linkages, and IT infrastructure requirements should all be considered. All essential stakeholders should have access to the plan, which should be documented.

Crisis Management and Response

Crisis management and response tactics should be included in business continuity planning. This entails putting together a crisis management team and specifying their roles and duties. The team should be prepared to respond effectively in the event of a crisis, which includes activating the business continuity plan, coordinating emergency response operations, and communicating with internal and external stakeholders. To ensure fast and accurate distribution of information, crisis communication protocols should be in place.

Backup and Recovery Systems

Backup and recovery solutions are an essential component of business continuity planning. Regular data backups, offsite storage, redundant IT systems, and alternative communication channels are all part of this. To set acceptable downtime and data loss levels, organizations should develop recovery time objectives (RTO) and recovery point objectives (RPO). Backup and recovery systems must be tested and validated on a regular basis to ensure their effectiveness during a real disruption.

Training and Awareness

Employee training and awareness are required for an effective business continuity plan. Employees should be familiarized with their roles and duties during a crisis through regular training sessions and simulations. This comprises procedures for emergency evacuation, communication protocols, and the utilization of backup systems. Awareness programs can help to build a preparation culture and ensure that staff understands the value of business continuity planning.

Testing and Exercising

It is critical to test and exercise the business continuity plan in order to discover any gaps or weaknesses and update the plan accordingly. This can include tabletop exercises, simulation exercises, or full-scale drills to evaluate the success of the strategy and the crisis management team's response. Lessons obtained from these activities should be documented and used to continuously update and improve the plan.

Continuous Monitoring and Improvement

Business continuity planning is a continual activity that necessitates constant monitoring and improvement. Periodic reviews and updates should be conducted by organizations to reflect changes in the business climate, technology, or risk landscape. This includes revising the risk assessment, updating contact information, assessing recovery strategies, and applying lessons learned from real-world occurrences or exercises.

Organizations can reduce the effect of disruptions and assure the continuity of important activities by adopting a solid business continuity plan. It enables them to respond to emergencies effectively, protect their employees and stakeholders, maintain customer trust, and ensure their long-term profitability.

HOW TO PREPARE FOR UNEXPECTED EVENTS

Preparing for unanticipated events necessitates a proactive and comprehensive approach that encompasses all parts of a company, including people, technology, and operations. Organizations can improve their readiness and resilience to deal with unexpected events by employing the following measures:

Risk Assessment and Scenario Planning

Conduct an in-depth risk assessment to identify potential hazards and their impact on various sections of the organization. Natural disasters, cybersecurity threats, supply chain disruptions, and public health concerns should all be considered in this assessment. Create scenarios based on these risks to better understand how they might play out and the potential repercussions. This data will serve as the foundation for future preparedness activities.

Business Continuity Planning

Create a detailed business continuity plan outlining the measures to be done in the case of an unforeseen incident. This strategy should contain measures for keeping critical processes running smoothly, ensuring employee safety, and communicating with stakeholders. During a crisis, identify vital functions, build backup systems and other locations, and specify roles and duties for key individuals. Review and update the plan on a regular basis to handle emerging risks and changing conditions.

Cross-Functional Training and Awareness

Provide training and awareness initiatives to staff at all levels and departments within the firm. Educate them on potential hazards, emergency response processes, and their roles and duties in the case of an unforeseen event. Create a preparedness culture and encourage staff to disclose any potential dangers or vulnerabilities they discover. Regular drills and simulations should be conducted to assess the effectiveness of preparedness measures and identify areas for improvement.

Communication and Crisis Management

Create a strong communication strategy for internal and external stakeholders during unforeseen situations. Define the communication channels, key spokespersons, and escalation procedures in detail. Make certain that all staff are aware of the communication protocols and have access to up-to-date contact information. To ensure consistent and timely communication, create pre-approved messages and templates for various scenarios. Monitor news and social media outlets to respond to disinformation as soon as possible.

Technology and Data Protection

Examine the organization's IT infrastructure and data security procedures to ensure they are resilient to unforeseen circumstances. To protect sensitive information, implement backup systems, data recovery procedures, and cybersecurity protocols. Update and test IT systems on a regular basis to uncover vulnerabilities and rectify any potential flaws. To ensure business continuity during a crisis, consider cloud-based solutions and remote access capabilities.

Supply Chain and Vendor Management

Examine and diversify the organization's supply chain to reduce disruptions caused by unanticipated incidents. Determine important suppliers and develop alternate sources or backup plans. Establish partnerships with secondary vendors to assure the availability of critical goods and services. Assess the financial health and risk profile of major vendors on a regular basis to mitigate supply chain risks. To be aware of potential disruptions, establish clear contact routes with suppliers.

Insurance and Risk Transfer

Collaborate with insurance providers to assess the organization's insurance coverage and ensure it is enough for any hazards. Consider purchasing additional coverage or adding riders to meet specific risks connected with unforeseen situations. Investigate risk- transfer possibilities via contractual agreements, such as indemnification clauses or force majeure provisions. Consult with legal professionals to better grasp the organization's liabilities and obligations in various scenarios.

Continuous Monitoring and Evaluation

Create a system for ongoing monitoring and evaluation of preparedness measures. Based on changing circumstances and developing risks, review and update risk assessments, business continuity plans, and communication protocols on a regular basis. Conduct post- event evaluations to identify key takeaways and areas for improvement. Stay informed about best practices and new trends in preparedness by connecting with industry networks, government agencies, and professional groups.

Organizations can improve their ability to navigate unforeseen occurrences by taking a proactive and integrated approach to preparedness. Remember that readiness is a continuous activity that involves continual review, adaption, and participation from all levels of the organization.

While organizations seek to monitor and predict various hazards, certain aspects can be difficult, if not impossible, to monitor and predict effectively. These uncertainties might represent serious dangers to a company. Let us look at a few examples:

Black Swan Events

Black swan events are unusual, unexpected events with catastrophic consequences that are impossible to predict using traditional forecasting methods. Natural disasters, economic crises, and technology disruptions are examples of unexpected events that can have far-reaching implications. Organizations may find it difficult to anticipate and plan for such disasters due to their unpredictable nature.

Rapid Technological Advancements

Technology is advancing at an unprecedented rate, bringing with it new hazards and opportunities. It can be difficult to predict the precise direction and impact of technological developments such as artificial intelligence, blockchain, or quantum computing. Organizations may find it difficult to predict how these advances may disrupt industries, introduce new dangers, or transform business strategies.

Regulatory Changes

Governments and regulatory agencies frequently enact new laws, regulations, or policies that have far-reaching consequences for industries and organizations. It might be difficult to predict the timing, extent, or specifics of regulatory changes. Organizations may encounter compliance risks or obstacles while modifying their operations to meet new regulations, particularly in industries with complex or rapidly changing regulatory environments.

Global Geopolitical Events

Political insecurity, economic disputes, and geopolitical crises can all have a significant influence on enterprises that operate in numerous nations. These occurrences are frequently unpredictable, and their outcomes can be unpredictable. Changes in government policy, trade obstacles, or societal instability in diverse locations may pose hazards to organizations with international operations.

Emerging Risks

As the world changes, new dangers develop that businesses may not have encountered previously. Examples include cybersecurity concerns, climate change-related hazards, and social media-related reputational risks. Because of their dynamic nature and the lack of previous data or existing risk management frameworks, identifying and assessing emerging risks can be difficult.

Human Behavior and Psychology

Human behavior and psychology can be complicated and unpredictable, presenting hazards that are difficult to quantify and successfully monitor. Employee misconduct, consumer sentiment, and public opinion can all have a substantial impact on a company's reputation and performance. Predicting and controlling risks associated with human behavior necessitates a thorough grasp of social dynamics as well as individual decision- making processes.

While these uncertainties pose difficulties, organizations can nevertheless take proactive actions to mitigate the risks associated with them:

1. *Develop a Resilient and Agile Culture*

   Create a company culture that values flexibility, resilience, and agility. This will allow the company to adapt to unforeseen events and manage uncertain situations more successfully.

2. *Scenario Planning and Contingency Strategies*

   Participate in scenario planning exercises to investigate several potential future scenarios and establish contingency plans. This enables companies to be better prepared to respond to and adapt to unforeseen circumstances.

3. *Foster a Learning Culture*

   Encourage internal knowledge-sharing and constant learning. This allows employees to stay up to date on developing trends and threats, allowing the firm to adapt and respond more effectively.

4. *Diversification and Redundancy*

   To mitigate the impact of unforeseen occurrences in specific regions or industries, consider diversifying activities, supply lines, or markets. Adding redundancy to important systems and processes can also help to reduce the risks associated with technical breakdowns or disruptions.

5. *Collaboration and Information Sharing*

   Create networks and collaborations with other organizations, industry associations, or governmental authorities to share information and collaborate on risk monitoring and management activities. Collective intelligence and shared resources can assist in more effectively addressing uncertainties.

It is critical to recognize that complete eradication of ambiguity is not achievable. Organizations, on the other hand, can improve their resilience and ability to respond to unforeseen events and uncertainties by taking a proactive and flexible approach to risk management.

CHAPTER 10

Mitigation

MITIGATION is the practice of decreasing or minimizing the impact of risks and potential undesirable outcomes. Mitigation of reputational risk entails developing strategies and activities to prevent or control circumstances that could impair an organization's reputation. Here are some main mitigating measures for minimizing reputational risk:

Proactive Reputation Management

Implement a proactive approach to reputation management by actively monitoring and assessing potential threats to the organization's reputation. Conduct regular reputation audits to identify weaknesses and areas for development. Create a complete reputation management plan that includes strategies, policies, and procedures for dealing with reputational threats successfully.

Strong Ethical Framework

Create and support a solid ethical framework within the organization. Clearly identify and explain the organization's values and code of behavior. Ensure that employees, management, and stakeholders understand the importance of ethical behavior and the potential influence on the organization's reputation. To encourage ethical actions, give ethics training and awareness initiatives on a regular basis.

Crisis Management Planning

Create a solid crisis management plan to effectively respond to reputational issues. Identify potential risks and scenarios that could hurt the organization's reputation, and define clear actions and responsibilities for crisis management and communication.

Designate crisis communication trained spokespersons to ensure quick and accurate messaging during crises.

Stakeholder Engagement

Develop and maintain solid relationships with important stakeholders like as customers, investors, employees, and the community. Engage with stakeholders on a regular basis to learn about their expectations, concerns, and feedback. Establish methods for open and transparent communication with stakeholders, addressing their requirements and proving the organization's commitment to their interests.

Employee Training and Engagement

Invest in extensive employee training programs to ensure that they understand their responsibility in protecting the organization's reputation. Provide instruction on ethical behavior, customer service, and crisis management. Encourage employees to take ownership of their activities and their impact on the organization's reputation by cultivating an engagement and empowerment culture.

Social Media and Online Presence Management

Manage the organization's online profile proactively, including social media platforms and online review sites. Monitor social media outlets for potential reputation issues and respond quickly to any unfavorable comments or disinformation. Create standards for appropriate online behavior for employees and establish consistency in messaging across online channels.

Continuous Improvement and Learning

Evaluating and reviewing the effectiveness of reputation management techniques and mitigation initiatives on a regular basis. Analyze previous events or near-misses to discover opportunities for improvement. Keep up to current on evolving trends, technology, and best practices in reputation management in order to adapt and improve the organization's risk mitigation methods.

Partnerships and Collaborations

Establish strategic alliances and cooperation with organizations that have a good reputation and share your beliefs. Alliances with respected entities can serve to improve the organization's reputation while mitigating the dangers associated with undesirable relationships.

Media Relations

Develop positive ties with media outlets and journalists. Engage the media actively to convey positive stories, accomplishments, and projects that correspond with the organization's values. Establish a reputation as a credible source of information and media guidelines for handling queries and interviews.

Monitoring and Early Warning Systems

Implement monitoring tools to detect early symptoms of reputational risk. Monitor media coverage, social media trends, and industry changes to uncover potential issues that may have an influence on the organization's reputation. Implement methods for employees and stakeholders to report potential hazards or concerns.

By employing these mitigation techniques, firms can effectively manage reputational risks and retain a positive reputation. Remember that reputational risk management is an ongoing activity that necessitates constant awareness and adaptation to new problems and opportunities.

What strategies can be employed to manage risks?

Several measures can be used to manage the risks connected with individuals in a company as well as reputational risk. Here are some effective risk-mitigation strategies:

Robust Recruitment and Selection Process

Implement a thorough and stringent recruitment and selection procedure to guarantee that only people with the necessary skills, qualifications, and values are employed. Conduct background checks, reference checks, and interviews to evaluate potential employees' character and integrity. The risk of unethical activity and reputational damage can be decreased by recruiting personnel who share the values of the firm.

Comprehensive Training and Development

Employees at all levels should receive extensive training to ensure they understand the organization's principles, ethics, and expected behavior. Diversity and inclusion training, ethical decision-making, and social media usage should all be included. Ongoing professional development opportunities can also help staff stay current on ethical standards while emphasizing the necessity of reputation management.

Code of Conduct and Ethics Policies

Create a strong code of conduct and ethics policies that define anticipated behavior, ethical standards, and repercussions for noncompliance. Distribute these policies to all employees and ensure that they understand

and accept them. Review and update these policies on a regular basis to handle emerging risks and changes in the business environment.

Whistleblower Hotline and Reporting Mechanisms

Set up confidential reporting methods, such as a whistleblower hotline or an anonymous reporting system, to encourage staff to report any unethical or improper actions. Ensure that staffs are aware of these tools and that they feel comfortable reporting problems without fear of retaliation. To maintain confidence and integrity within the organization, evaluate and rectify any reported issues as soon as possible.

Leadership Accountability and Transparency

Encourage accountability and transparency culture throughout the organization, beginning with leaders and executives. Leaders should set a good example, follow ethical guidelines, and be open about their decision-making processes. To create confidence among employees and stakeholders, encourage open communication, regular updates, and transparent reporting.

Stakeholder Engagement and Relationship Management

Engage with stakeholders, including customers, suppliers, and investors, to learn about their expectations, concerns, and criticism. Communicate with stakeholders on a regular basis and respond to their wants and concerns as soon as possible. During difficult circumstances, building strong connections based on trust and openness can help limit reputational risks and increase stakeholder support.

Crisis Management and Communication Plan

To effectively respond to reputational crises, create a complete crisis management and communication plan. Identifying potential dangers and scenarios, developing communication channels, and preparing critical messages are all part of this process. During a crisis, timely and honest communication can help to limit reputational harm and sustain stakeholder confidence.

Continuous Monitoring and Risk Assessment

Implement a continuous monitoring system to identify new threats, assess their potential influence on reputation, and take proactive mitigation actions. Monitor social media sites, news channels, and industry trends to stay current on public opinion and respond quickly to any emerging difficulties. Conduct regular risk assessments to identify areas of vulnerability and put risk mitigation methods in place.

Online Reputation Management

Actively maintain the organization's online profile by monitoring social media, responding to customer comments, and addressing undesirable information as soon as possible. Create a strategy for encouraging good online involvement, sharing useful and reliable information, and establishing a solid online reputation. Engaging customers and stakeholders via digital platforms can aid in mitigating reputational risks posed by online sources.

Continuous Improvement and Evaluation

Evaluate the effectiveness of risk mitigation techniques on a regular basis and change them as needed. Conduct internal audits, get input from employees and stakeholders, and assess the effectiveness of reputation management programs. Continuous improvement and learning from prior experiences will assist firms in properly mitigating risk and protecting their brand.

Organizations can proactively manage risks related to people and reputational hazards by applying these techniques, thereby protecting their reputation, and developing trust among stakeholders.

ENTERPRISE RISK MANAGEMENT

ERM is a comprehensive and systematic strategy for detecting, assessing, and managing risks across an entire organization. It entails putting in place a systematic framework and processes for proactively identifying potential risks, analyzing their potential impact, and putting in place suitable risk response plans. ERM seeks to improve an organization's capacity to fulfill its goals while reducing the negative impact of risks on its operations, reputation, and overall performance.

ENTERPRISE RISK MANAGEMENT ESSENTIALS

Identifying Risks

The first stage in ERM is to identify and categorize any risks that could jeopardize the organization's goals. This entails a systematic method of obtaining information, conducting risk assessments, and involving stakeholders to ensure a thorough awareness of hazards across the company.

Risk Assessment and Analysis

Once discovered, risks must be evaluated and studied to determine their possible impact and likelihood. This step entails assessing the magnitude of each risk, comprehending its drivers and potential effects, and quantifying risk exposure. Risk assessments can be carried out using either qualitative or quantitative methodologies, or a combination of the two.

Risk Evaluation and Prioritization

The assessed hazards are analyzed in this step to determine their priority for future action. Risks are frequently prioritized based on their possible impact and likelihood while taking the organization's risk appetite and tolerance levels into account. This aids in directing resources and efforts toward addressing the most serious risks that could have a significant impact on the organization's goals.

Risk Assessment and Treatment

Risk response strategies are established and implemented after risks have been identified and prioritized. This entails establishing the most effective risk-management strategy for each risk, which may include risk avoidance, risk reduction/mitigation, risk transfer, or risk acceptance. Risk response methods are intended to reduce the likelihood and impact of hazards, while also aligning with business goals and optimizing resource allocation.

Risk Assessment and Reporting

ERM is a continuous process that necessitates continuous risk monitoring and tracking. Regular monitoring aids in the identification of changes in the risk landscape, the evaluation of the effectiveness of risk mitigation strategies, and the detection of emerging hazards. To assist decision-making and transparency, organizations build reporting procedures to convey important risk information to key stakeholders such as management, board members, and external parties.

Strategic Planning and Decision-Making Integration

When ERM is integrated into an organization's strategic planning and decision-making processes, it is most effective. Organizations can integrate risk management activities with their overall aims and objectives by assessing risks at the strategic level. This integration aids in recognizing potential risks connected with new business initiatives, investments, or changes, enabling for more informed decision-making.

THE ADVANTAGES OF ENTERPRISE RISK MANAGEMENT

ERM provides a structured way to consider risks in decision-making processes, allowing firms to make informed choices that balance risk and reward.

- Enhanced resilience: Organizations can improve their ability to endure and recover from disruptive events by proactively recognizing and addressing risks.

- Cost reduction: Effective risk management assists firms in optimizing resource allocation by focusing on the most critical risks and minimizing needless costs connected with risk incidents.

- Stakeholder trust: Demonstrating a strong ERM framework helps boost stakeholder trust, including investors, regulators, and customers, by demonstrating the organization's commitment to risk management.

- Competitive advantage: Organizations with effective ERM processes are better positioned to navigate uncertainties, capitalize on opportunities, and achieve a competitive advantage in the marketplace.

In essence, Enterprise Risk Management is a comprehensive methodology that helps organizations systematically discover, assess, and manage risks. Organizations can improve their ability to achieve goals, preserve assets, and navigate uncertainties in an increasingly complex business environment by embracing ERM concepts and practices.

AVOID / REDUCE / ADJUST / SHARE / ACCEPT

The risk response or risk treatment framework, also known as the Avoid/ Reduce/Adjust/Share/Accept framework, provides a systematic strategy for organizations to address identified hazards. It assists companies in making informed decisions about how to respond to hazards based on their possible impact and probability. Let us take a closer look at each framework component:

AVOID

The "Avoid" technique entails taking steps to reduce or eliminate the danger. This could mean stopping some operations, not pursuing specific projects, or leaving markets where the risks outweigh the possible advantages. When the risk is deemed intolerable and there are feasible alternatives available to meet corporate goals, avoidance is often used.

REDUCE

The "Reduce" strategy seeks to mitigate risk by putting in place measures that reduce the likelihood or impact of a risk event. This may entail putting in place control mechanisms, enhancing processes, or using new technologies to mitigate the risk's possible consequences. Redundancy systems, safety regulations, training programs, and supplier diversification can all be used to reduce reliance on a single source.

ADJUST

The "Adjust" technique entails modifying the organization's activities or processes to accommodate the risk without totally removing or minimizing it. This method is frequently utilized when avoiding or reducing the risk is impossible or impractical. Modifying corporate processes, adjusting policies or procedures, or implementing contingency plans can all help to lessen the impact of a risk when it occurs.

SHARE

The "Share" technique entails passing some of the risks to a third party. This can be accomplished through insurance policies, contracts, or partnerships in which risk management is shared. Sharing the risk can help to divide the financial burden or skills required to successfully address the risk. Organizations must evaluate the feasibility and cost-effectiveness of sharing risks with third-party stakeholders.

ACCEPT

The "Accept" technique entails recognizing and actively deciding to bear the risk in the absence of specified risk reduction measures. This method is often used when the potential impact of the risk is small or when the cost of mitigating the risk outweighs the projected benefits. Acceptance does not indicate indifference; rather, it entails monitoring the danger and preparing to respond if the risk materializes.

It is essential to note that the best risk response plan will rely on the specific risk, its context, and the organization's risk appetite and tolerance levels. A variety of techniques may also be used to address various hazards within the firm.

Organizations should examine and reassess their risk landscape on a regular basis to ensure that the risk response techniques they have chosen are acceptable and successful. Furthermore, the framework should be integrated with the larger Enterprise Risk Management (ERM) processes to create a consistent and unified risk management approach.

Organizations may make well-informed decisions about how to handle risks, limit potential impacts, and optimize resource allocation to achieve their objectives while managing uncertainties by employing the Avoid/Reduce/Adjust/Share/Accept framework.

CHAPTER 11

Risk Remedies

RISK remedies are activities done to handle identified risks and limit their possible impact on a business. They are also known as risk response methods or risk treatment choices. After identifying and assessing risks, companies can select from a variety of risk remedies based on the nature of the risk, the organization's risk appetite, and the available resources. Here are some common risk-reduction strategies:

Risk Avoidance

Eliminating or avoiding activities or events that pose a major risk to the organization is what risk avoidance entails. This can be accomplished by avoiding high-risk activities, withdrawing specific products or services, or avoiding collaborations with high-risk firms. When the potential consequence of the risk outweighs the benefits of accepting the risk, risk avoidance is a successful technique.

Risk Reduction or Mitigation

The goal of risk reduction is to reduce the likelihood or impact of a danger. This can be accomplished by putting in place control mechanisms, best practices, and safeguards. Implementing safety protocols, improving security measures, conducting frequent inspections, or implementing redundancy systems are all examples of risk mitigation tactics. Organizations hope to limit the potential negative repercussions by lowering the risk level.

Risk Transfer

Transferring the financial or operational weight of a risk to a third party is what risk transfer entails. This can be accomplished using insurance policies, contracts, or outsourcing arrangements. Organizations transfer risk when they transfer responsibility for managing and covering the repercussions of a risk to another party. It is crucial to stress, however, that the organization retains responsibility for overseeing and assuring the success of the risk transfer arrangement.

Risk Acceptance

Accepting a risk entails knowingly admitting its presence and opting not to take any specific action to mitigate it. This method is often used when the expense or effort of risk management surpasses the risk's potential impact. Certain hazards may be accepted by organizations if they are within their risk appetite and can be controlled within acceptable limitations. Risk acceptance does not imply completely dismissing the risk, but rather making an informed decision to endure it.

Risk Diversification

Risk diversification, often known as financial risk management, entails spreading risks over multiple regions, projects, or investments. Organizations decrease their exposure to a single risk source by diversifying their portfolios or operations. This strategy seeks to balance risk and possible returns while reducing the impact of a single risk on the business.

Contingency Planning

Contingency planning is creating a specified reaction plan that will be implemented if a specific risk event occurs. Contingency plans detail the activities that will be taken, the resources that will be required, and the responsibilities that will be assigned in response to the risk occurrence. This method enables firms to respond quickly and efficiently to unanticipated risk events while maintaining key operations.

It is critical to emphasize that the risk remedies chosen should be based on a thorough study of the risks and their potential consequences, considering the organization's risk appetite, resources, and strategic objectives. To address distinct components of a risk, a mix of risk remedies may be required. Continuous monitoring and evaluation of risk management strategies are also required to ensure their continued efficacy and relevance in a dynamic corporate environment.

Risk Culture

Risk culture is important in risk management because it shapes an organization's response to hazards and its capacity to manage them effectively. Risk culture refers to an organization's values, beliefs, attitudes, and behaviors that impact how risks are perceived, acknowledged, and addressed at all levels.

A strong risk culture develops an atmosphere in which risk management is built into the DNA of the organization and everyone understands their roles and responsibilities in detecting, analyzing, and mitigating risks. It encourages open communication, and proactive risk-taking, and emphasizes accountability for risk management.

When addressing risk culture, keep the following elements in mind:

Leadership and Tone at the Top

>The risk culture of a business begins at the top. Leaders are critical for setting the tone and demonstrating a commitment to risk management. Employees are more likely to follow leaders that prioritize risk management and display ethical behavior.

Risk Awareness and Education

A good risk culture necessitates that employees comprehend risk concepts and their implications. Companies should invest in risk awareness programs and provide comprehensive training to all levels of staff. When confronted with hazards, this enables individuals to make educated judgments and take appropriate action.

Risk Appetite and Tolerance

Establishing a clear risk appetite—the level of risk a business is ready to accept to achieve its goals—is part of risk culture. This should be in line with the strategic aims and values of the firm. Employees should be aware of their risk tolerance levels and make decisions accordingly.

Open Communication and Reporting

A good risk culture encourages employees to disclose risks and near-misses through open and transparent communication channels. This allows for the early detection and reduction of dangers. Encouraging discussions about risks and lessons learned contributes to the development of a culture of continuous improvement.

Incentives and Recognition

Positive risk culture can be reinforced by aligning incentives and recognition systems with effective risk management methods. Individuals and teams who are recognized and rewarded for their contributions to risk management encourage proactive risk detection and foster a sense of responsibility.

Integration into Decision-Making

When risk management becomes an inherent component of decision-making processes, risk culture is enhanced. Organizations may make better decisions and prevent unnecessary risk exposure by weighing risks and potential rewards.

Continuous Monitoring and Adaptation

Risk culture is a continual process that involves constant monitoring and adjustments. Regular evaluations, audits, and reviews aid in the identification of gaps and opportunities for development. Organizations must be adaptable in order to adapt their risk culture to changing internal and external circumstances.

Creating a strong risk culture requires time and effort, but the rewards are substantial. A robust risk culture improves organizational resilience, decreases surprises, and positions the organization to effectively negotiate uncertainty.

Organizations may promote a risk-aware mindset, enable individuals to take ownership of risks, and ultimately improve their ability to achieve strategic objectives while effectively managing possible threats and opportunities by establishing a positive risk culture.

An Effective Compliance Program

An effective compliance program is critical for firms to ensure conformity to relevant laws, regulations, and ethical standards. It is a proactive strategy for identifying and mitigating risks connected with non-compliance, unethical behavior, and potential legal ramifications. Organizations can foster a culture of honesty, openness, and responsibility by developing an effective compliance program.

Key Elements of an Effective Compliance Program:

Written Policies and Procedures

To aid employees in understanding and complying with applicable rules and regulations, clear and thorough policies and procedures should be implemented. These documents should be examined and updated on a regular basis to reflect changes in the regulatory environment.

Leadership and Tone at the Top

Senior management is crucial in establishing the tone for organizational compliance. Their commitment to ethical behavior and compliance should be clearly communicated throughout the organization at all levels, highlighting the importance of compliance and the repercussions of non-compliance.

Risk Assessment

Regular risk assessments aid in identifying potential areas of compliance weakness. Understanding the specific risks that the company faces allows suitable controls and mitigation methods to be created to successfully handle those risks.

Training and Education

Ongoing training and education initiatives are critical for raising compliance awareness and ensuring staff understand their roles. Relevant laws and regulations, company rules, ethical behavior, and reporting methods for any infractions should all be included in the training.

Communication and Reporting Channels

It is critical to establish open lines of communication and provide clear avenues for reporting any compliance infractions or concerns. Employees should feel comfortable reporting any suspected wrongdoing without fear of retaliation.

Monitoring and Auditing

Regular compliance monitoring and auditing aid in determining the efficacy of the compliance program. Conducting internal audits, examining critical processes, and adopting controls to detect and prevent noncompliance are all part of this.

Investigation and Response

A well-defined process for investigating reported infractions is essential for an efficient compliance program. Prompt and thorough investigations are required to resolve possible violations, implement appropriate disciplinary actions, and prevent recurrence.

Continuous Improvement

Compliance programs must be flexible and adaptable to changes in the regulatory environment. Regular review, feedback, and continuous improvement activities help to increase the program's effectiveness over time.

The Advantages of an Effective Compliance Program

Risk Mitigation

A successful compliance program assists in identifying and mitigating risks associated with noncompliance, so avoiding legal penalties, reputational harm, and financial losses.

Ethical Culture

A strong compliance program develops an organizational culture of integrity, ethical behavior, and responsible business practices.

Regulatory Compliance

Organizations can assure compliance with applicable laws and regulations by maintaining up-to-date on evolving rules and industry standards, lowering the likelihood of infractions and the accompanying consequences.

Stakeholder Confidence

A strong compliance program increases stakeholders' faith in the organization's commitment to ethical behavior, resulting in a positive reputation and trust among customers, investors, and partners.

Improved Decision-Making

Compliance programs give employees the knowledge and assistance they need to make educated decisions that are in line with legal and ethical obligations.

Early Detection and Resolution

Potential compliance concerns can be recognized and resolved early with proper monitoring and reporting processes in place, limiting their impact and preventing escalation.

An effective compliance program is critical for firms navigating complicated regulatory landscapes, mitigating risks, and upholding ethical standards. Organizations can safeguard their reputation and ensure long-term success by adopting and sustaining such a program, which fosters a culture of compliance, honesty, and accountability.

CHAPTER 12

Risk Auditing

Rısk auditing is an essential component of good risk management and plays a significant role in guaranteeing the integrity, dependability, and openness of financial reporting, as well as the overall governance and control processes inside a company. Auditors can identify and assess possible risks, evaluate existing controls, and provide important insights and recommendations to management by performing risk-focused audits.

In the context of auditing, risks are any variables or occurrences that have the potential to undermine an organization's ability to achieve its goals. Internal procedures, external market conditions, technology improvements, legislative changes, and other factors can all contribute to these risks. The primary purpose of risk auditing is to analyze the effectiveness of an organization's risk management framework and control environment, as well as to provide confidence that risks are being discovered, assessed, and mitigated adequately.

KEY ASPECTS OF RISK AUDITING

Risk Assessment
- Auditors must be well-versed in the organization's risk management framework and practices.
- They detect and assess risks by considering the underlying risk profile, the control environment, and the impact on financial statements and operations.

- Gathering relevant information, interpreting data, and using risk assessment procedures are all part of risk assessment.

Internal Controls Evaluation

- Auditors evaluate an organization's internal controls for their efficacy in minimizing recognized risks.
- They assess control design and execution, test their operational efficacy, and detect control flaws or defects.
- Internal controls are critical in risk management, assuring the correctness and dependability of financial data, and preventing fraud and errors.

Compliance with laws and regulations

- Risk auditing entails evaluating the organization's adherence to applicable laws, regulations, and industry standards.
- Auditors examine policies, processes, and internal controls to ensure that legal and regulatory requirements are met.
- They also evaluate the organization's ability to identify and respond to emerging regulatory risks and business environment changes.

Audit Planning and Execution

- The audit strategy is created based on the risks that have been identified and their significance.
- Auditors choose the right audit procedures, such as sample selection, interviews, observations, and data analysis methodologies.
- They collect evidence and conduct testing procedures to evaluate the effectiveness of controls and discover any control flaws or gaps.

Reporting and Communication

- Auditor findings and suggestions are communicated to management, the board of directors, and other stakeholders.

- Audit reports provide an objective assessment of risks, control inadequacies, and improvement possibilities.

- Clear and succinct communication assists management in effectively understanding and addressing risks, supporting informed decision-making.

Continuous Monitoring and Follow-up

- Risk auditing is a continual activity, and auditors may be involved in continuous monitoring operations.

- Auditors may support management in establishing and implementing risk mitigation plans, as well as monitoring their progress.

- Follow-up audits may be performed to evaluate the efficacy of corrective activities implemented in response to recognized risks and control inadequacies.

Risk auditing necessitates auditors having a thorough awareness of the organization's industry, operations, and risk landscape. It is also necessary to have a solid understanding of auditing standards, risk management frameworks, and relevant legal requirements. Auditors use their skills to assist firms to improve their risk management capabilities, establishing internal controls, and protecting their reputation and financial stability.

Finally, risk auditing is an important part of risk management because it ensures that firms have effective procedures in place to identify, analyze, and reduce risks. Auditors assist firms preserve trust, improve decision-making, and manage the intricacies of an ever-changing risk environment by offering objective and impartial assessments.

Role of Internal Audit

Internal audit is an essential component of an organization's governance structure and plays a critical role in risk management. It delivers significant insights and recommendations to improve risk management processes, internal controls, and overall organizational performance as an independent and objective assurance function. Internal auditing entails numerous critical responsibilities:

Risk Assessment and Management

Internal auditors' help firms discover and assess risks in numerous areas of operation. They assess the efficacy of existing risk management systems, policies, and procedures and make suggestions for improvement. Internal audit, through conducting risk assessments, assists firms in prioritizing risks, determining risk appetite, and developing risk mitigation strategies.

Compliance and Regulatory Requirements

Internal auditors guarantee that businesses follow all applicable laws, regulations, and industry standards. They evaluate the efficacy of internal controls and ensure that policies and procedures are followed. Internal auditing assists in identifying areas of noncompliance and making recommendations to correct any inadequacies, hence lowering the risk of legal and regulatory fines.

Internal Control Evaluation

Internal auditors assess the adequacy and effectiveness of an organization's internal controls. They evaluate the design and execution of control systems with the purpose of preventing and detecting fraud, mistakes, and inefficiencies. Internal audit helps to strengthen internal control frameworks and mitigate risks related to financial reporting, data security, and operational processes by identifying control deficiencies.

Operational Efficiency and Effectiveness

Internal auditing assists businesses in optimizing their operations by assessing efficiency and effectiveness. Internal auditors discover chances for improvement, cost savings, and process streamlining by analyzing processes and procedures. Their observations and recommendations help to improve operational performance and achieve company goals.

Fraud Detection and Prevention

Internal auditors are critical in detecting and preventing fraud within a company. They discover red flags, anomalous transactions, and control holes that may suggest fraudulent activity through independent and impartial assessments. The internal audit makes recommendations to improve anti-fraud measures and assists with investigations when fraudulent activity is detected.

Stakeholder Communication and Collaboration

Internal auditors serve as a conduit for communication between management, the board of directors, and other stakeholders. They ensure transparency and accountability by communicating audit results, recommendations, and progress reports to all parties involved. Internal audit encourages collaboration by collaborating with management to address risks and improve organizational performance.

Continuous Improvement

Internal auditing fosters a culture of continual improvement inside a company. They monitor and evaluate the success of recommended activities by conducting regular audits and assessments. Internal auditors also keep up to current on emerging risks, industry trends, and best practices, and can offer advice on how to improve risk management techniques.

Internal audit, in summary, is a critical role that gives objective and independent assurance on risk management, internal controls, compliance, and operational efficiency.

Its job extends beyond financial auditing to include a wide variety of activities to assist businesses in managing risks, protecting assets, and effectively achieving their goals.

CHAPTER 13

Bribery and Corruption

CORRUPTION refers to the abuse of entrusted power for private gain. Corruption may be committed by public officials who abuse the authority of their public office for personal gain, which interferes with democracy and the rule of law.

Corruption may also be committed by private individuals who abuse their positions for personal gain, which can hinder fair market operations and distort competition.

Facilitation payments are those made to a foreign official to expedite or secure routine government action. Corruption, bribery, and other fraudulent activities undermine public trust in political and economic institutions and leaders, threatens economic and social development, hurts fair trade, and exposes organizations and their employees to risks including legal, financial, and reputational. As per the UK Bribery Act 2010, bribing a public official is a crime. Bribery cases may involve Foreign Public Officials or other influential government officers.

An organization must be committed to the prevention, deterrence, and detection of fraud in all its forms, including bribery and corruption. In line with the aims of anti-bribery and anti-corruption laws including the FCPA and the UK Bribery Act, organizations are required to prohibit direct and indirect payments of anything of value to obtain or retain business or to secure any improper advantage.

Corruption includes money laundering, tax evasion, bribery, fraud etc.

Bribery of government officials is a significant corruption risk and prohibited under most local laws of different jurisdictions. Under the United States Foreign Corrupt Practices Act (FCPA), a "government official" has been very broadly construed. All interactions with government officials must comply with this Policy, the organization's Code of Conduct, and with all applicable laws, rules, and regulations. All such interactions must adhere to the Board and Management's commitment to act in compliance with this policy and the highest ethical standards considering doing business honestly and legally.

All employees and third parties should not create the appearance of impropriety regardless of whether there was any improper intent. The organization's employees and management shall ensure that gifts, hospitality, or entertainment are not provided to government officials, however, if required, then written pre-approval by the Compliance Officer or other appropriate representative shall be required in every instance when gifts, hospitality, travel, or entertainment is to be offered or extended to a government official.

Facilitation payments are a type of bribe made to a foreign official to expedite or secure routine government action. While in some countries they are customary, in others, they are improper. Under the FCPA, it is a narrowly defined term that refers to certain small expediting, or "grease," payments that, while not illegal, must be properly controlled and recorded on a company's books. Facilitating payments are illegal under the laws of most countries around the world. In keeping with this policy of compliance with all applicable laws, the organization must not permit facilitating payments. If an employee receives a request for facilitating payment, the employee should decline to make it. It is not permissible to make such payments during the course of the employee's work for the organization, even if that employee bears the cost of such payments personally and does not seek reimbursement.

Why Do Corruption Exist?

There is no single reason behind the occurrence of corruption. Whenever corruption-related incidents occur, there is a need to look at the situation from the perspective of the person who committed the act of bribery or corruption. It is necessary to consider the following factors:

- the motivation of persons who committed the bribery and corruption and the conditions under which they rationalized their behaviour
- the opportunities available to commit bribery and corruption
- the technical and power ability of the person who committed the bribery and corruption
- the expected risk of discovery of the bribery and corruption activities after they have been performed
- the consequences of bribery and corruption such as penalties, punishments, etc.

Corruption often occurs due to a combination three factors, which are outlined below. They often occur together which tells us that bribery and corruption cases usually result from a combination of factors. These three factors are as follows:

- Aspect
- Motivation
- Cause and Trinity

Below are the bribery and corruption-related factors in more detail:

Aspect

> The aspect may be the motivation which is based on either greed or the need of the person committing the bribery and corruption. Greed continues to be the main cause of fraud in many countries

and jurisdictions. Many people are faced with or provided with the opportunity to commit bribery and corruption.

The personality, knowledge, and temperament of a fraudster enables them to confidently commit frauds – they are not timid or scared individuals. There is also the possibility that good people fall into the bad company of criminals who make them commit bribery and corruption in the workplace or the companies where these good people are employed.

For example, a bank employee may be used by the criminal to transfer the money from one location to another through opening an account with the bank, without any due diligence of the criminal. The purpose may be the performance of bribery and corruption.

Opportunity

Bribery and corruption usually occur in companies where there is a weak system of internal controls and in which poor security measures are implemented. Fraudsters exploit the weak internal control system and commit the activities to gain benefits.

Establishing robust internal controls is the responsibility of the Board of Directors and Senior Management of the company. Without appropriate and robust processes and controls, the operations of the company or organizations may not be run, causing various losses to the company such as operational, reputational, and financial losses. The financial position of the company deteriorates without appropriate internal controls.

A weak internal controls system means weak governance structure and poor policies and processes. Due to the weak internal control system, the organization is exposed to various types of risks, such as:

- Financial risk
- Reputational risk

- Operational risk
- Legal risk
- Regulatory risk
- Strategic risk etc.

Cause and Trinity

Bribery and corruption may occur due to a lack of knowledge and awareness about the applicable laws and regulations. Most of the people committing corruption and bribery are unaware of the potential consequences, therefore, they do not realize the impacts that may have occurred on their professional image and reputation. Various people obey the laws and regulations of the country because they believe that compliance with laws and regulations is their main responsibility. These types of people are afraid of being exposed if they are found in any illegal activity or non-compliance with any law or regulation.

However, some people may be able to rationalize fraudulent acts and actions as:

- necessary – especially when done for the business
- harmless – because the victim is large enough to absorb the impact
- justified – because "the victim deserved it' or because "I was mistreated"

The consequences of bribery and corruption are the punishments as per the applicable regulatory framework and the compliance policies of the organization. The employees may be issued with show-cause notices from the human resource department and they may also be terminated from employment due to their involvement in bribery and corruption. Some organizations have a zero tolerance regarding corruption therefore, the employees and related persons have their employment terminated immediately.

CHAPTER 14

Fraud

THE term "fraud" usually includes activities such as theft, corruption, embezzlement, money laundering, bribery, insider trading, and extortion.

All fraudulent activities are illegal and any person or persons involved in these activities are categorized as criminals. In other words, using deception to dishonestly make a personal gain for oneself and/or create a loss for another is fraud.

Experts say that "fraud is not a possibility; it is a reality" as companies and businesses are always dealing with several suspicious incidents on a more or less permanent basis.

Fraud is usually an intentional act or series of acts of tricky and cunning, using two types of misrepresentations which are a suggestion of falsehood or suppression of truth.

It is primarily the responsibility of management to establish systems and controls to prevent or detect fraud, errors, and weaknesses of internal controls. These systems and controls may then be monitored by the internal audit department. Internal audit may also be required by management to specifically review the entity's exposure to error or fraud or to undertake a special investigation to look into suspected error or fraud.

Although fraud is prevalent across organizations of all sizes and in all sectors and locations, research shows that certain businesses are exposed to greater levels of fraud risks than others, such as banks, money service businesses, money transfer businesses, manufacturing businesses, etc. Their control environments should be adjusted to fit with the degree of fraud risk exposure.

Below are some examples of activities that are considered fraudulent activities:

Counterfeiting

Counterfeiting is one of the examples of fraud incidents or fraud types that may result in significant and extreme financial consequences for the organization. The use of emerging and new technology by the fraudsters enables them to counterfeit and produce realistic-looking materials and packaging to fool legitimate traders including wholesalers and retailers.

Counterfeiting is considered a lucrative business activity for the fraudster, which provides tremendous avenues and possibilities of making large commercial profits through the utilization of technology. It is a problem affecting a wide range of industries including pharmaceuticals, electrical goods, and fashion. However, there are often many victims affected by such fraud and not just the business that has been duped or had their brand exploited.

Theft of plant

Employees or staff of the company may be involved in the theft of the plant and assets. Employees usually take advantage of access to the plants and assets and steal those assets to gain financial benefits or money. The theft of the plant and assets owned by the company are considered fraud.

Inventory or cash

Employees or staff of the company may be involved in the theft of the inventory items or the cash. Employees often take advantage of access to the inventories and cash and steal them to gain financially in the form of the readily availability of cash.

The theft of the inventories and cash is considered fraudulent activity. Inventory theft cases occur in companies or organizations which are involved in manufacturing goods and theft of cash usually occurs in banks or institutions where access to cash holding is common for the authorized staff.

False invoicing

False invoicing methods are used by the employees of the company to make wrong or excess payments to outsiders or vendors. Such vendors may be involved with the employees of the company in order to commit fraud. Through false invoicing, the wrong payments are released to the vendors, who in turn provide financial benefits to the concerned employees of the company that made false invoicing.

There are also situations where false payments are made to the vendors or suppliers who are owned by the employees of the company themselves.

For example: Mr. A of company ABC may be involved in false invoicing, where he makes various false payments to the supplier of stationery items, which is owned by Mr. A himself.

Money laundering

Criminals transfer their illegal funds from one place to another, through the use of a country's financial system such as banking channels. Transfer of illegal money may be to support other criminals in various other jurisdictions or countries.

Money laundering activities are considered both fraudulent and illegal activities. Different types of organizations are exposed to money laundering risks such as banks, payment service providers, money transfer organizations, real estate, stock market, etc.

Payroll fraud

Payroll fraud is related to the concept of "ghost employees"; Companies or employees commit these types of fraud to transfer the funds of the company in the name of employees who are not the real employees of the company or those who are not hired. Payroll fraud involves running monthly payroll and making salary payments to the employees who are not actually on the payroll of the company.

This type of fraud is common in very large organizations which employ thousands of employees in various cities throughout a country. Payroll fraud is planned and performed by the human resource department of the organization or company.

In mid-sized organizations or companies, this type of fraud may be performed by the finance personnel who are authorized to manage and run the monthly payroll or salaries disbursements.

What is the Scale of the Problem?

In the past various attempts have been made to measure the scale of fraud, but compiling reliable statistics around incidents of fraud is not easy. As one of the key characteristics of fraud is trickery or deception, it is usually very difficult to identify the scale of the problem.

The reality is that most fraudulent incidents are not identified or go undetected and, even when fraudulent activity has been identified, it may not be appropriately or timely reported. One reason for this may be that a company that has been a victim of fraud does not want to take the burden of reputational losses and in order to suppress the reputational risks, the fraudulent activities and cases are not reported publicly. Companies also face challenges in distinguishing between fraud and carelessness. Carelessness may be the poor accounting records or not recording financial transactions on a timely basis causing working capital issues.

There is no doubt that fraudulent elements are present in almost every organization, which is a serious issue. Research and survey results may not give a complete picture about it, but companies might be able to deny that fraudulent elements are present if the cases are not reported.

Various incidents of fraud go undetected and actual losses and indirect costs to the business such as management costs or damage to reputation, which may be significant, are not highlighted which also suppress the scale of fraud in a particular country, state, or industry. Therefore, it is difficult to put a total cost on fraud based on any survey or related results.

For example, if one of the fraud surveys reports highlights that fraud results in losses of $20 billion each year in the US and another report highlight that corruption and bribery cases aggregate 5% of the value of the world economy or about $2.00 trillion per year, then estimates are not comparable because the survey focus points are not same and they also exclude other types of fraud such as misappropriation of assets.

It may be impossible to calculate the total cost of fraud, but fraud is considered to be very significant than the total cost of various other illegal activities or crimes. We may depict the significance of fraud through the fact that in terms of causing harm to society or an economy the fraud is second to drug trafficking.

One of the misconceptions about fraud is that it is a victimless crime, however, the fraud cases and incidents may have various types of psychological and social effects on individuals, companies, and society.

For example, when a significant fraud case is identified it usually destroys the reputation and strategic mission of the company, and numerous individuals including employees and other related businesses or stakeholders are affected.

In addition to the employees, working in a company where significant fraud is identified and reported, employees of the suppliers can be affected because of future orders. Other stakeholders such as creditors, including banks, are indirectly affected due to non-payment of timely instalments against the loans obtained by the company where the significant fraud case is reported.

The cost of the fraud is usually transferred to the consumers by charging a premium for goods and services, to compensate for the costs of fraud losses which include fraud amount, cost of investigations, and additional security costs.

Due to fraud activities, the resources of the society as a whole are drained, which significantly affects the public services. Fraud also involves supporting other criminal or money launderers in different jurisdictions, which also pose a risk of reputational and strategic losses for the economy of the country.

Which Businesses are Affected?

Fraud is an issue that all businesses or companies may face regardless of their nature of business, size of operations, industry, or jurisdiction. To run the business affairs, companies or businesses need various resources such as people, cash, goods, information assets, or services from various vendors, therefore, the possibility of fraud attempts are increased.

There is a myth that fraudulent activities have occurred only in large companies or multinational companies, which are reported on in the media, and that small companies or businesses are unlikely to be a target of fraudsters.

Small businesses suffer fraud more frequently than large businesses or companies and are hit by higher average losses, often because of weak internal controls system or poor hierarchy. When fraudulent cases are reported in smaller companies, they are less likely to be able to cover up the damages as compared to a larger business or company and may go bankrupt.

In the past various surveys have shown that companies which reported frauds were working in many different industries and the industries most suffered from fraudulent activities and losses were insurance and industrial manufacturing.

Significant fraud losses also occur in the financial services industry, such as banks and other financial institutions because of the large amount of cash and property dealings through these organizations. Even not-for-profit organizations (NPOs) are also victims of fraud cases. These organizations are exploited by the money launderers or criminals for placement of their funds and generate more wealth from the general public by showing them social cause and issues and gain their sentiments.

Fraud Costs

Fraud carries associated cost which extends beyond monetary value. The cost of fraud includes reputational, operational, and regulatory costs. Companies and businesses face hard and soft costs associated with the fraud.

The hard costs are considered as a measurable cost which may include a consumers' loss of goods and/or services, and/or merchants' loss of sales.

The soft costs are not easily measurable and may include reputational impacts for the consumer, operational and regulatory impacts for the company, and vendors such as merchants.

Measuring fraud and error costs

To run the business affairs, the organizations and companies perform cost analysis and prepares cost budgets, which are made part of the overall company budget. Companies know their cost structures which include various types of costs, such as:

- staffing costs
- accommodation costs
- utility costs
- procurement costs
- salaries costs
- security and administration etc.

Managing these costs requires detailed analysis at the time of estimating future costs, to improve the efficiency of business and operations.

The process of estimating the business and operations costs include the assessment of expected fraud incidents and related costs. Fraud and error costs estimations may show significant amounts which if not appropriately addressed may lead to not only financial losses to the company but the chances of occurrence of reputational and regulatory losses also increase significantly.

No estimation of fraud cost by the companies may be due to the denial of the fact that fraud may occur in the future as no such instances were identified and reported in the past. This unrealistic prediction by any company may lead to not accounting for the cost of fraud in business operations cost estimations leading to significant financial losses.

A cost can only be reduced by the business if it is accurately or reasonably measured, therefore estimating the fraud cost is necessary for any business or company to ensure that appropriate measures are taken to reduce the impacts of fraud occurs.

When a company knows the extent of the possible fraud losses, then it comes into a better position to manage those possible fraud costs, to ensure that the financial health and stability of the company or business is maintained.

CHAPTER 15

Data and Information

Understanding Data and Information

DATA is a raw form of information, and it lacks proper meaning or usefulness, unless it is processed and transformed into some meaningful form. Data is defined as individual facts, while information is the organization and interpretation of those facts.

Information is a processed form of data, which is developed or formed to arrive at a particular decision or to use in taking some decisions.

Organizations capture data and information from various internal and external sources. The data needs to be analysed and understood, in order to convert it into some meaningful form. For example, data might be the number of customers, who opened their accounts with a financial institution. This data is not meaningful, unless it is analysed and divided into smaller pieces to make the data more meaningful. The divided form of data may be called as the information.

Data is not useful unless transformed into information. Data must be captured from the reliable and legitimate sources, in order to ensure that the information which is generated from the data, is useful for the organization. If the data is not captured from a reliable source or the data is not correct or complete, then the information shall also be incomplete or meaningless, which may lead to wrong decisions.

Understanding Corporate Data and Information

Corporate data or information means the data or information captured by the organization, from various sources, for example data or information related to general market research performed before launching a new product. Companies capture data or information from internet, regulators websites, media portals, directly from business customers, etc. This corporate data is meaningless, unless appropriately analysed and transformed into useable information. Organizations use data or information for various purposes, including decision making in different areas such as product expansion, market expansion, closure of business segments, setting budgets for the year, estimating revenues and expenses, and checking compliance with laws and regulations.

Examples of corporate data and information include, customer data, statistical data, vendors information, inventory record, passenger data etc. The precise need of data varies from organizations to organizations. The data useful for a financial institution may be useless for the manufacturing company.

Corporate data information management is a critical area in an organization because without having relevant and complete data or information, an organization may not perform review of the performance and assess the risks faced by the business and operations. Importance of maintaining corporate data or information is increased because regulatory authorities require organizations, to identify, classify and record it in a meaningful and appropriate form.

Management and recording of corporate data or information depend on the working style of the organization, such as some organizations have a culture of managing information centrally or some may process or record in a decentralized manner.

Understanding Decentralized Data

Decentralized data is an emerging trend due to the involvement of technology to secure the stored data or information.

When we talk about the cryptocurrencies and other digital assets, we get to know about the concept of decentralized finance or DeFi, which eliminates intermediaries by allowing people, merchants, and businesses to conduct financial transactions through emerging technology. This is accomplished through peer-to-peer financial networks that use security protocols, connectivity, software, and hardware advancements. The system removes the control banks and institutions have on money, financial products, and financial services. Some of the key attractions of DeFi include that:

- It eliminates the fees that financial institutions charge for using the services.

- People hold money in a secure digital wallet instead of keeping it in an institution such as a bank.

- People can use the internet connection without needing approval.

- People can transfer funds in seconds and minutes.

Decentralized finance tokens provide crypto users with access to several bank-like services such as loans, lending, and insurance. Defi tokens represent a diverse set of cryptocurrencies native to automated, decentralized platforms that operate using smart contracts. Decentralized finance, or DeFi, uses emerging technology to remove third parties in financial transactions. The components of DeFi are stablecoins, software, and hardware that enables the development of applications. The infrastructure for DeFi and its regulation are still under development and debate. In the centralized finance for financial institutions, the money is held by banks, whose goal is to make more money.

Why is Data or Information Stored as Decentralized More Secure?

Corporate data or information which is stored in a decentralized manner is considered as more secure because such data or information is not controlled by anyone person or system. Example of data or information stored in a decentralized manner is the data or information stored in the Blockchain technology.

Decentralized corporate data or information is more secure due to no central point of control. Hackers would not find it easy to attack the stored data or information stored in a decentralized form. The data or information spread across the network with blockchain technology, is more protected from tampering. For example, users can use blockchain technology to create a decentralized database that is secure and free from hacks or data breaches.

CHAPTER 16

Understanding Criticality of Information and Data/Information Fraud

What Data or Information is Critical?

CRITICAL data or information refers to the type of information that organizations can use to take strategic decisions and formulate business strategy. For example, the personal information of customers, business and working data related to vendors, regulatory data in the form of laws and regulations implemented by regulatory authorities, financial data, target market information, data about operational losses occurred in previous periods, and so on.

The critical data or information requires prevention from data or formation fraud. The term 'fraud' usually includes activities such as theft, corruption, embezzlement, money laundering, bribery, insider trading, and extortion. All fraud activities are illegal and person or persons involved in these activities are categorized as criminals. In other words, using deception to dishonestly make a personal gain for oneself and/or create a loss for another is Fraud. Experts say that "Data or Information Fraud is not a possibility; it is a reality" as companies and businesses are always dealing with several suspicious incidents on a more or less permanent basis. Fraud usually is an intentional act or series of acts which is perpetrated by human beings using trickery, and cunning using two types of misrepresentations which are a suggestion of falsehood or suppression of truth.

It is primarily the responsibility of management to establish systems and controls, to prevent or detect fraud, errors, and weaknesses of internal controls. These systems and controls may then be monitored by the internal audit department. Internal audit may also be required by management to specifically review the entity's exposure to error or fraud or to undertake a special investigation to look into suspected error or fraud.

Although fraud is prevalent across organizations of all sizes and in all sectors and locations, research shows that certain businesses are exposed to greater levels of fraud risks, than others, such as banks, money service businesses, money transfer businesses, manufacturing businesses, etc. The control environment should be adjusted to fit with the degree of fraud risk exposure with layers of security measures, necessary to protect the real form and ensure availability for corporate decision-making purposes. Misuse or loss of critical data or information may result in the imposition of significant fines and penalties, by the relevant regulatory authorities.

In order to prevent data losses and financial implications, regulatory authorities prescribe security measures, including cybersecurity measures, defining data access related authority levels, identifying authorized and unauthorized people, knowing the purpose of accessing data before use or access, prevention of taking or using corporate and critical data or information out of the organization, reviews of information systems and networks for possible misuse of cybersecurity related threats, etc.

Loss of critical data or information results in the loss of reputation, which cause customers to lose confidence with the organization and they start switching their relationships with other more secure organization, offering similar services or products.

For example, if a cyberattack occurs in a financial institution, which resulted in compromise of critical data of its customers, then the customers will lose confidence in that financial-institution. Customers will start closing their accounts, and switch to other technology enabled and more secured financial institution.

Data Fraud Indicators

Fraud indicators are alerts which trigger the investigation process to be performed by management or the fraud investigation team. Fraud indicators help management in highlighting risk factors, which must be monitored and investigated when occurred.

Organizations focus on the protection of data losses through the "Data Loss Prevention" measures to ensure that data losses, data breaches, exfiltration, or unwanted destruction critical data is detected and prevented. Organizations use data loss protection measures, to protect and secure internal data and comply with applicable data protection regulations. The Data Loss Prevention term refers to defending organizations against data leakage, where important data is lost, such as due to the occurrence of a cyber-attack. Data loss prevention is related to prevention of illicit transfer of data outside organizational boundaries.

The common causes of data leaks include:

- Insider threats where an attacker who has compromised a privileged user account, abuses their permissions and attempts to move data out of the organization.

- Extrusion by attackers in which attackers penetrate the security perimeter using techniques like phishing, malware or code injection, and gain access to sensitive data.

- Unintentional or negligent data exposure occur as a result of employees who lose sensitive data in public, provide open Internet access to data, or fail to restrict access per organizational policies.

There are various fraud indicators which when identified may require initiation of the fraud investigation process. When we talk about financial statements fraud, the following are some of the circumstances examples that may indicate the possibility that the financial statements may contain a material misstatement resulting from fraud:

- Transactions that are not recorded in a complete or timely manner or are improperly recorded as to amount, accounting period, classification, or entity policy.
- Unsupported or unauthorized balances or transactions.
- Last-minute adjustments significantly affect financial results.
- Documents that appear to have been altered.
- Unavailability of other than photocopied or electronically transmitted documents when documents in original form are expected to exist.
- Significant unexplained items on reconciliations.
- Unusual balance sheet changes, or changes in trends or important financial statement ratios or relationships – for example, receivables growing faster than revenues.
- Evidence of employees' access to systems and records inconsistent with that necessary to perform their authorized duties.
- Tips or complaints to the auditor about the alleged fraud. Conflicting or missing evidence, including:
- Missing documents.
- Missing inventory or physical assets of significant magnitude.
- Unavailable or missing electronic evidence, inconsistent with the entity's record retention practices or policies.
- Inconsistent, vague, or implausible responses from management or employees arising from inquiries or analytical procedures. θ Unusual discrepancies between the entity's records and confirmation replies.
- Large numbers of credit entries and other adjustments were made to accounts receivable records.

- Unexplained or inadequately explained differences between the accounts receivable sub

- Missing or non-existent canceled checks in circumstances where canceled checks are ordinarily returned to the entity with the bank statement.

- Fewer responses to confirmations than anticipated or a greater number of responses than anticipated.

- Inability to produce evidence of key systems development and program change testing and implementation activities for current-year system changes and deployments.

Based on the identification of data or information fraud indicators, the fraud investigation process is initiated which requires appropriate planning at the very initial stages of the investigation. Careful planning and the right strategy may not only help in the identification of the real culprit but also recover the amounts which are embezzled by the suspect. The larger-scale fraud incidents are often international, where the frauds activities span over different jurisdictions. Therefore, fraud investigation planning must include elements of taking legal and investigative actions across different jurisdictions and borders. In such types of frauds where cross-border criminals are involved, the involvement of law enforcement authorities and agencies becomes necessary. The international level frauds cause significant harm to organizations and even the country. Various professionals, experts, and experienced criminals usually combine in international frauds and it becomes difficult for the fraud examiner to rightly get to the root cause and real fraudsters.

Every country and jurisdiction has different laws and regulations, which are required to be complied with by the people and citizens. For international level frauds, the authorities of relevant countries should collaborate and identify the fraud trial for the identification of real culprits. An example may be where the money launderers transfer their black money from one country to another to support the criminals in different jurisdictions.

This happens with the involvement of the professionals working in the organization, who combine with the money launderers to provide them access to the financial system of the organization. To investigate the fraud case, the planning process covers various important elements such as suspect interviews, seeking legal advice, taking legal actions, and police referral.

In today's digital environment, the audit trail is maintained by the companies and organizations in the form of electronic records by using personal computers and other electronic devices such as PDAs. In the electronic environment, the data or information fraud or manipulation investigation team or experts perform computer forensic investigations, by the seizure and analysis of electronic data using a methodology that ensures its admissibility as evidence in a court of law.

Legislations allow the use of computer forensic investigations, as an important part of the whole fraud investigations because it has an impact on an organization's ability to investigate computer systems and electronic records such as email. Organizations are required to maintain electronic records and information appropriately and over a specified period as per the applicable regulatory requirements. Such record maintenance enables and facilitates in performing the appropriate fraud investigations by the experts.

In computer forensics, the original information or data is never altered. To ensure this, the purpose-written 'forensic image' software is used by the fraud investigation teams, to obtain a copy of a 'target' computer system. The forensic image enables recreation of the original system at any time.

To ensure confidentiality of the company's information it must be ensured that the fraud investigation team is an experienced specialist which must ensure confidentiality of information assets. Computer forensic investigators and other supporters who gather evidence from the computers must be able to justify their actions in the future. It is strongly recommended that a forensics expert is hired for professional advice rather than relying solely on the company's information technology department or staff. Forensic computer images have been accepted in the legal proceedings and it is no longer required (in most cases) to seize computer hardware for investigations purposes.

Indeed, in situations where target computer systems contain critical data, the physical seizure may not be a viable option for the fraud investigations team. The forensic image may be sufficient and the need to seize physical assets may not arise. Forensic imaging also enables the drawing of the information from the suspect's personal computer without conducting inquiries from the suspect directly.

CHAPTER 17

Information Security

Information Security Objectives

ORGANIZATIONS need to protect data, data resources and information systems from the manipulation and unauthorized data access. Critical data that must be protected include, personally identifiable information, protected health information, personal information, intellectual property, data, and governmental and industry information systems.

Organizations need to safeguard the critical data or information, to ensure the smooth functioning of the business and operational activities. Organizations therefore, set guidelines for data and information security through understanding and addressing the following minimum objectives:

- Commitment to IT Security
- IT Security Risk Management
- Implementation of IT Security Policy
- Data and Information Security Awareness & Training

The objective is to increase IT Security awareness of the organizations, and secondly to implement guidelines to formulate an effective institution-wide technology security framework, to protect their valuable information, and resources.

The guidelines provide a starting point to set policies and procedures in place that will eventually reduce the likelihood of internal or external attack on IT resources and limit the damage caused by an inadvertent or malicious incident.

Information Security Governance and Supervision

Commitment to data and information security, a clear direction towards IT Security Risks Management practices, and implementation of IS Security policy measures, is required in organizations, to avoid the data or critical information losses, data misuse or data manipulation.

Organizations set up IT Governance, and supervision practices in the form of establishing a dedicated IS Security management committee, which oversee the use of technology and resources, to support business and operational objectives. The committee provides guidance in designing and modifying the policies to cope with the IT and information risks, documenting issues, and initiatives, and monitoring the team's performance. The committee may be a mix of personnel from the senior management, including business heads and IT senior officers, and they should meet on periodic basis, and document the minutes of the meetings.

When an organization performs transactions, it is prone to data loss or misuse risks. The risk and control mechanism and policies are evolving to restrict this information security risks, to an acceptable level. The success of an IT Security program depends on its effective practices and measures around the risk management. With a proper security risk management, an organization can identify, assess, measure, monitor information security risks, and take appropriate actions to reduce them. As more and more products & services become technology driven, and reliance on technology assets, the more are the risks the organizations must face

The regulatory authorities recognizes that financial industry is built around trust and the sanctity of the financial transactions. Owing to the critical role of organizations and institutions, and the extreme sensitivity of their information resources and information assets, the seriousness of

IT Security, and the ever-increasing threats, which they face cannot be overstated. As more and more products & services become technology driven, and reliance on technology assets, the more are the risks the organizations must face. Regulatory authorities recognizes that financial industry is built around trust and the sanctity of the financial transactions. Owing to the critical role of organizations and institutions, and the extreme sensitivity of their information resources and information assets, the seriousness of IT Security, and the ever-increasing threats, which they face cannot be overstated.

CHAPTER 18

Hacking, Data Manipulation, and Data Losses

What is Hacking, Data Fraud and Data Loss

HACKING is the unauthorized access to the servers, networks, information systems or applications used by an organization, to manage its business and operational activities. Hackers are outsiders, who plan to penetrate the networks of an organization, to gain access to the confidential or critical information of the organization. Critical information may include customers personal information, internal strategic information, or any other sensitive data or information, stored in the information systems or servers of the organization.

Data fraud or data manipulation involves alteration or misuse of data by internal or external stakeholders. Employees may gain access to data or information and alter that either intentionally or unintentionally, causing financial and reputational losses to the organization. False invoicing is an example of data manipulation and it is performed by the employees of the company to make wrong or excess payments to outsiders or vendors. Such vendors may be involved with the employees of the company, to commit fraud. Through false invoicing, the wrong payments are released to the vendors, who in turn provide financial benefits to the concerned employees of the company that made false invoicing. There may also be situations where false payments are made to the vendors or suppliers who are owned by the employees of the company themselves. For example,

Mr. C of company XYZ may be involved in false invoicing, where he made various false payments to the supplier of stationery items, which is owned by Mr. C himself.

In the past various attempts have been made to measure the scale of fraud, but compiling reliable statistics around the fraud is not easy. As one of the key characteristics of fraud is trickery or deception, therefore, it is usually very difficult to identify the scale of the problem.

It is a reality that the majority of frauds are not identified or go undetected and, even when a fraud has been found, it may not be appropriate or timely reported. One reason for this may be that a company that has been a victim of fraud does not want to take the burden of reputational losses and to suppress the reputational risks the fraud instances and cases are not reported publicly. Companies also face challenges in distinguishing between fraud and carelessness. Carelessness may be the poor accounting records or not recording financial transactions on a timely basis causing working capital issues.

There is no doubt that fraud elements are present in almost every organization which is a serious issue. The researches and survey results may not give a complete picture about it, but we may not deny that fraud elements are not present if the cases are not reported.

Various frauds go undetected and actual losses and indirect costs to the business such as management costs or damage to reputation, which may be significant, are not highlighted which also suppress the scale of fraud in a particular country, state, or industry. Therefore, it is difficult to put a total cost on fraud based on any survey or related results. It may be impossible to calculate the total cost of fraud, but fraud is considered to be very significant than the total cost of various other illegal activities or crimes. We may depict the significance of fraud through the fact that in terms of causing harm to society or an economy the fraud is second to drug trafficking.

One of the misconceptions about fraud is that it is a victimless crime, however, the fraud cases and incidents may have various types of psychological and social effects on individuals, companies, and society. For example, when a significant fraud case is identified it usually destroys the reputation and strategic mission of the company, and numerous individuals including employees and other related businesses or stakeholders are affected. In addition to the employees, working in a company where significant fraud is identified and reported, employees of the suppliers can be affected because of future orders. Other stakeholders such as creditors, including banks, are indirectly affected due to non-payment of timely instalments against the loans obtained by the company where the significant fraud case is reported.

The cost of the fraud is usually transferred to the consumers by charging a premium for goods and services, to compensate for the costs of fraud losses which include fraud amount, cost of investigations, and additional security costs. Due to fraud activities, the resources of the society are drained, which significantly affects the public services. Fraud also involves supporting other criminal or money launderers in different jurisdictions, which also pose a risk of reputational and strategic losses for the economy of the country.

Data manipulation may also be related to payroll fraud, such as "ghost employees." These types of frauds are committed to transfer the funds of the company in the name of employees who are not the real employees of the company. Payroll fraud involves running monthly payroll and making salary payments, to those who are not on the company payroll. This is where the data manipulation and payroll fraud are planned and performed by the human resource department of the organization or company. In mid-sized organizations or companies, this type of fraud may be performed by the finance personnel, who are authorized to manage and run the monthly payroll or salaries disbursements.

Data loss means the loss of control over the data, due to a particular data loss incident or change caused by unauthorized data access and use practices. Data loss may be caused by the mistake or errors of the employees or it may also be intentional. Intentional data loss may be to gain the personal financial advantages by stealing the data and control over it and passing it to some competitor.

How Can the Data Hacking and Manipulation Be Prevented?

The Board of Directors are primarily responsible to provide appropriate oversight to the employees, to manage the entity and activity level risks, including cybersecurity risks and threats. Cybersecurity governance gives a strategic overview of how an organization develops, and implements internal security controls to ensure security of information assets and information systems, including defining the cybersecurity risk appetite, establishing information security committee to oversee the threats and cybersecurity risks, building ownership levels and accountabilities.

Data or information hacking or cyberattacks may be prevented through the implementation of appropriate information security measures and practices, including performing IS Security risk assessment and management, performing regular data, information and information systems reviews, and regular testing of system vulnerabilities to external data or information loss threats. Hackers after getting the access to the information, steal it, and demand ransom money from the organization to restore the stolen information. Cyberattacks cause the employees to not able to access their systems and information, leading them to static state, where they are at the mercy of the hackers, who gained the control over their systems and application.

Cybersecurity is the practice of protecting systems, laptops, computers, networks, servers, electronic devices, information, and data from possible malicious attacks by the hackers. Cybersecurity is also known as information security or information technology security. Purpose is to maintain the integrity and privacy of data. Cybersecurity covers user data access rights and users are required to take permissions, when accessing any information source.

Cybersecurity practices include the development and maintenance of a robust data/information recovery, and business continuity plans, to minimize the effects of unauthorized data access by hackers. Security measures and risk management practices define how the organization shall respond to a possible cyberattack incident, to avoid loss of information, data, or resources.

Data losses may also be incurred due to viruses injected into the information system. End-user awareness, and education address unpredictable cybersecurity risks and threats, because anyone in the organization can cause introducing a virus in the network or system, by failing to follow security measures and practices, implemented in the organization, and expected to be complied with by the users. Education, for example include requiring users to not open or delete the suspicious emails or email attachments, not using unidentified USB drives in systems, etc.

Who Commits Data or Information Fraud

Understanding fraudsters is an important part of assessing the risks of fraud in any organization or company. Understanding the fraudsters helps in analyzing the reasons why people or fraudsters commit the frauds. In most cases, frauds occur because people are allowed to do so. Companies and organizations face a wide range of threats and the threat of fraud can come from inside or outside of the organization.

Fraud specialists have long debated whether it is possible to develop a profile of a fraudster that is accurate enough to enable organizations to catch people in the act of fraud or even beforehand. A strong analysis of possible frauds and the fraudsters may help the companies and organizations to strengthen their lines of defense against criminal activities.

Companies should know that the fraud may not be committed if the potential fraudster believes that the achievable rewards will only be modest and the chances of detection are high or that the punishment set for a particular type of fraud is very high. The main way to assess the fraudsters' motives and attitude toward fraud is to establish a system where management may assess in detail the possible fraudulent threats and from whom the threats are coming in. This assessment leads a company to judge the likelihood of occurrence of the fraud.

Data or information fraudsters usually fall into one of three categories:

Pre-planned data fraudsters intend to commit fraud from the beginning and may be short-term fraudsters, such as those who use stolen credit cards to gain financial benefits or may use false social security numbers. They may also be long-term players, who may be involved in bankruptcies cases or they may be involved in serious crimes such as money laundering activities.

Intermediate data fraudsters are the fraudsters who in the beginning work as honest employees or individuals but turn to fraud when times get hard, such as frustration at being passed over for promotion or experiencing family challenges

Slippery-slope data fraudsters are the fraudsters who are simply involved in trading businesses objectively. They are not able to pay their debts to run the affairs of the business.

The type of fraudster is continually changing. One major change is due to the rapidly growing use of technology by companies and fraudsters. New techniques of fraud are emerging and companies need to respond to these techniques by updating their line of defences. The use of the technology has enabled many data or information fraudsters, to perform frauds from remote locations. These types of data or information frauds are occurring in both the technologically advanced, and other developing countries. A major concern for all businesses is that the younger generations are more able to use new technology and have access to much more data or information. This makes companies and businesses more vulnerable, as data knowledge makes fraudsters to perform targeted attacks on the data or information assets of an organization.

By analysing this fact, usually, it becomes possible for the companies and businesses to go beyond to respond to various unforeseen fraud instances and develop strategies to pre-empt and minimize fraud losses. It is intended to provide the reader with insights into the relationship between the attributes of fraudsters, their motivations, and the environment in which they flourish. Data or information fraudsters are generally acting against their organizations, and may mostly be employed in an executive role, or other functions such as finance, operations, supply chain and sales/ marketing.

Data or information fraudsters are educated and technically sound people, committing the data manipulation in a very sophisticated manner. Understanding the characteristics and circumstances of data or information fraudsters is very important both for planning the activities to meet any possible data fraudulent activities or investigating fraud incidents. Most of the fraudsters are employed by the victim organization for more than 6 to 10 years. Amongst the data or information fraudsters, employees may also commit data or information frauds, such as misappropriation of information assets, which is very common and covers a large percentage of total fraudulent activities, performed in a company or an organization. Understanding the behaviour of employees is crucial to identify the main causes of data or information fraud incidents, in a company. Another most prevalent type of data or information fraud involves, misreporting of revenues or overvaluation of assets in the financial management system.

CHAPTER 19

Cyber Security and Information Security Measures

What is Cybersecurity and Information Security

CYBERSECURITY is the practice of protecting systems, laptops, computers, networks, servers, electronic devices, information, and data from possible malicious attacks by the hackers. Cybersecurity protects all categories of data from the theft and damage, including sensitive data, personally identifiable information, protected health information, personal information, intellectual property, data, and governmental and industry information systems.

Some of the benefits of cybersecurity measures are as follows:

- Protect networks and data from unauthorized data access.
- Improved information security and business continuity planning and management.
- Improved confidence of employees and customers.
- Improved credibility of the organization because of necessary cybersecurity controls placed by organization to protect critical data or information.

Cybersecurity is also known as information security or information technology security. Purpose of cybersecurity of information security is to maintain the integrity and privacy of corporate data. Cybersecurity covers user data access rights, and establishing permission rights where users are required to take prior permissions, when accessing any data or information system or source.

Cybersecurity measures cover the development and maintenance of a robust disaster recovery, and business continuity plan, to minimize the effects of cyberattack incident and it defines how the organization shall respond to the cyberattack incident, to avoid loss exposure to information, data, or operations.

The eight essentials of cybersecurity are:
- application control,
- patch applications,
- configure Microsoft Office macro settings,
- user application hardening,
- restrict administrative privileges,
- patch operating systems,
- multi-factor authentication and
- regular backups

The appropriate cybersecurity approach has multiple layers of protection measures which are spread across the systems, computers, networks, programs, or information that an organization intends to keep safe. In organizations, the people, systems, and processes, should complement one another to defend the organization and its critical information resources, from the occurrence of possible cyber-attacks.

End-user awareness, and education address unpredictable cybersecurity risks and threats, because anyone in the organization can cause introducing a virus in the network or system, by failing to follow security measures and practices, implemented in the organization, and expected to be complied with by the users. Education, for example include requiring users to not open or delete the suspicious emails or email attachments, not using unidentified USB drives in systems, etc.

Cyber Incidents Threat Factors

Cyber incident threat actors are groups or individuals who, with malicious intent, aim to exploit weaknesses in an information system or exploit its operators to gain unauthorized access to or otherwise affect victims' data, devices, systems, and networks, including the authenticity of the information that flows to and from them. The globalized nature of the Internet allows threat actors to be physically located anywhere in the world and still affect the security of information systems.

Cyber incident threat actors can be categorized by their motivations and, to a degree, by their sophistication. Threat actors value access to devices and networks for different reasons, such as siphoning processing power, exfiltrating or manipulating information, degrading the network's performance, and extorting the owner. Some threat actors conduct threat activity against specific individuals or organizations, while others opportunistically target vulnerable systems. In general, each category of cyber threat actor has a primary motivation.

Cyber incident threat actors are not equal in terms of the sophistication and capability. They have a range of resources, training, and support for their activities. Cyber threat actors may operate on their own or as part of a larger organization. Sometimes, sophisticated actors use readily available tools and techniques because they can still be effective for a given task and/or make it difficult for defenders to attribute the activity. An example includes, leveraging the commercial security tools used by security researchers.

Advanced persistent threats (APT) refer to threat actors in the top tier of sophistication and skill. APTs can use advanced techniques to conduct complex and protracted campaigns in the pursuit of their goals. This designator is usually reserved for nation-states or very proficient organized crime groups.

Cybercriminals are primarily financially motivated and vary widely in sophistication. Organized crime groups often have planning and support functions in addition to specialized technical capabilities that can affect a large number of victims. Illegal online markets for cyber tools and services have made cybercrime more accessible and allowed cybercriminals to conduct more complex and sophisticated campaigns.

Insider threats are individuals working within their organization who are particularly dangerous because of their access to internal networks that are protected by security perimeters. Insider threats are often disgruntled employees, and may be associated with any of the other listed types of threat actors.

Data Fraud Detection

Data fraud detection is a review process that involves the review of historical financial transactions and other related information, to identify the fraud indicators in a particular department or function of the company. It involves the analysis of various conditions that highlight the fraud enablers, breaches of internal controls, and any possible management bias for the actual fraud incident.

One of the data frauds is the credit card fraud, including offline and online frauds. Offline fraud is committed using a stolen physical card at storefront. In most of the cases, the institution issuing the card can lock it before it is used in a fraudulent manner. Online fraud is committed via web, phone, or shopping, for which only card's detail is needed, and a manual signature is not required at the time of purchase.

The fraud detection process is also a forward-looking activity to assess the possibilities of reoccurrence of fraud incidents. To assess the reoccurrence of fraud in the future in any particular department or function of the company, the fraud investigators or experts analyze the historical as well as current fraud incidents, to establish the inter-connections between them. This connection assessment helps in the prediction of possible future fraud incidents.

To detect the fraud all the processes and activities are studies to find the controls weaknesses and possible avenues, which are exploited by the persons or data fraudsters. Data or information fraud detection is an ongoing process that is performed on the occurrence of fraud incidents or to assess the possibilities of occurrence of fraud in any particular area of the department.

Methods of Data or Information Fraud Detection

In most cases, the frauds are not detected by preventative or detective measures, but rather are identified through external or independent business functions or sources. Below are some methods of fraud detection, which identify the frauds:

Fraud Database

The management may establish a database built to record the details of fraud incidents, including the details of the progress of investigations. Such databases must be analyzed and monitored on an ongoing basis. This helps management in understanding the reasons and causes of fraud incidents, therefore, management establishes and implements relevant processes and procedures to prevent the occurrence of similar frauds. Therefore, management may predict the next possible occurrence of fraud incident in particular process or department through which possible fraud incidents or already occurred frauds are identified.

Internal Tip-off

The organization should establish the internal fraud deterrence processes with the element of the internal tip-off, to ensure that the fraud incidents are reported confidentially to the relevant department or authorities such as the fraud investigations department or the fraud management committee. Tip-off helps in planning the fraud investigation process without getting the culprit being informed. Such practices help in the performance of appropriate planning and performance of fraud investigations.

External Tip-off

The organization should establish the external corporate communication function where fraud-related external tip-off considerations are practiced, to ensure that the fraud incidents are reported to the organization by the stakeholders, in a confidential manner. External stakeholders might be the customers, general public, vendors, or regulators of the organization. Such communication from external stakeholders should be reported to the fraud investigations department or the fraud management committee.

Whistleblowing Hotline

Through a whistle-blower program, the organization demonstrates its commitment to good corporate governance and the establishment of a fraud risk management culture that promotes a high degree of ethics and belief in its stated corporate values. The data fraud identification policy highlights the responsibility of the employees to report any identified fraud to the senior management of the company. Usually, employees feel the reluctance to share the information with the management in the fear of losing their jobs, therefore, the senior management should devise a policy where everyone in the organization or company is encouraged to share the information with the senior management without any fear. The management may establish the fraud hotlines, as a means of encouraging the employees to report fraud incidents, without any fear.

Fraud identification process may include:

- encouraging the reporting of fraud incidents

- allowing for the appropriate investigation of the reported fraud incidents
- protecting employees who disclosed the frauds to the management

Communication and training

The management must ensure that appropriate training is provided to the employees for the prevention and detection of fraud incidents. The training programs should be developed based on the complexities of the operations of the organization. Training programs should be very practical and focused on the requirements to identify and prevent fraud in the organization. Every employee should be encouraged to identify the frauds in their respective departments and functions. The employees may be encouraged through awarding the prizes if the fraud incidents are identified and reported.

Law Enforcement Investigation

Law enforcement authorities investigate the frauds, where applicable legal provisions are breached. Law enforcement authorities perform a variety of tasks such as a collection of pieces of evidence and testifying the shreds of evidence in the relevant courts.

Law enforcement authorities may work for the Federal Government or the State. Police departments may also be involved in the fraud investigation process depending on the local applicable laws of the State and Federal Government. There may be situations where Law Enforcement Agencies and Police may work together undercover. The nature of the investigation and involvement of Agencies and Police depend on the location of fraud, size of the organization, profile of the fraudsters, and the legal provisions breached.

Internal Audit

The internal audit department of the organization is an independent function that reports to the Board Audit Committee. The internal audit function is headed by Chief Internal Audit, which is vested with the powers to investigate the fraud incidents and they are provided with sufficient authority to obtain and review the relevant shreds of evidence both within and outside the organization. Internal auditors appropriately plan the fraud investigations and deploy relevant and experienced resources to investigate the case. The process may involve interviewing the fraudsters and other relevant employees.

External Audit

External auditors of the organization are responsible for the performance of the audit of the financial statements of the company. Their scope is limited to the financial statements of the organization. However, there may be the possibility that management of the organization prepares the financial statements fraudulently or artificially inflate or deflate the financial amounts. External auditors are required to obtain sufficient appropriate audit evidence to support the audit opinion on the financial statements of the organization or company. To, cover the risk that financial statements may be prepared fraudulently, the external auditors appropriately plan the external audit. External auditors ensure that appropriate audit procedures are performed on the financial statements, balances, and amounts so that any intentional fraud is identified during the audit activities.

Data Fraud Investigations

To investigate the data frauds organization, use different tools and methods and deploy fraud investigation team or experts to perform:

- Investigations

- Data assessment and data mining
- Data analysis

The utilization of the above methods depends on the nature and severity of the business operations and fraud incidents. The investigation tools and techniques are discussed below:

Organizations face a severe loss of revenue due to fraud. To survive in the market, organizations usually offer a variety of data mining techniques for fraud detection. The fraud incidents continue to happen due to lack of data governance and data protection controls, which lead to the loss of revenue to the company. In this situation, the remedy to overcome data losses and fraud incidents is using data mining techniques and statistical tools to identify the cause of data fraud in advance and to take mitigation efforts. It involves the analysis of past history of the customers. Organizations generate and maintain a large volume of data and need to ensure the scope for the application of data mining techniques in databases maintained.

Forensic technology investigation

Transaction analysis or forensic audit is an important component of the fraud investigation process. Transaction analysis is performed by quantified and experienced professionals.

It becomes a challenge when the fraud suspects are themselves, skilled accountants, or professionals, with sound knowledge of the internal controls, processes, and the financial system of the company. Forensic accountants will be needed to analyse the activities in such types of organizations, where such types of professional fraudsters work. Forensic accountants not only analyse the activities of professional fraudsters but also calculate the estimated losses and damages caused by the fraudulent acts of professional and skilled fraudsters.

The search, seizure, and analysis of the electronic evidence, which is stored in personal computers or information devices are utilized and used as computer forensic investigations. Computer forensic data can also be obtained from remote locations where cloud services are used by the company. The forensic investigators get access to the financial and other information virtually to analyse and assess the evidence and information.

It is rare for modern-day fraud incidents to be identified without the use of data storage devices and computers, and due to these reasons, computer forensics is a vital skill-set.

The important part of the fraud investigations is the fieldwork and the interviews of the persons and suspects which can prove to be the conclusive evidence process. Information obtained during the interviews can become sufficient appropriate evidence.

Data Intelligence

Organizations use various smart intelligence bases processes and systems with the ability to perform the investigation process. Such systems are based on Artificial Intelligence. All the activities are tracked and analysed through the appropriate AI bases algorithms. Fraud investigation experts use such AI-based investigation tools and systems, to identify the real cause and culprits involved. Artificial intelligence can be used to enhance information security across the number of business departments and operations sections of the company, such as at retail and financial payments points or gateways. These AI-based intelligent fraud detection and investigation tools are used in those types of companies, which provide money services or payment services, to merchants and customers.

Data Analytics

Due to a large number of customers, financial transactions, and related information flow between different departments, it becomes difficult for organizations to understand and manage the data flow.

In data fraud investigations, understanding the data or information flow between different departments and stakeholders is very crucial. It is not practical for human beings or investigation team to analyze whole data or information flow, especially the complex data or information flow, without the use of any specialized methods or tools.

Data analytics help management and fraud investigation team to analyse the large data sets, to understand and identify the fraud risk or data fraud trends and indicators, related to different processes and departments of the company. A computer forensic technician or data analytic experts are employed by the companies to understand the large and complex data especially the data highlighting fraud indications or control lapses. Organizations and companies analyse the large amounts of data to investigate the frauds through different techniques, such as:

- data mining and data analysis
- database repositories including electronic data
- big data analysis or complex data analysis using materiality thresholds
- social media posts
- media news feeds
- sales, marketing, and operations materials

For example, the large number of financial transactions data of the company may be analysed better with data analytic tools such as Power BI. Finance professionals with fraud investigations experience utilizes intelligent tools and techniques to understand the linking of the financial data and transactions of the company. Process owners' access rights and recording of financial information by the relevant authorized persons are easily identified through the data analysis and tools.

CHAPTER 20

Understanding Risks and Information Security Risks

Cybersecurity or Information Security Risks

RISK means the possibility of occurrence of a negative incident, which if occur would result in negative consequences or loss of resources. Risks are of different types and categories including:

- Operational Risks
- Cybersecurity or Information Security Risks
- Financial Risks
- Regulatory Compliance Risks
- Reputational Risks, etc.

Risk is the likelihood of a negative occurrence or event happening and its consequences. In simple terms, risk is a combination of the chance that something may happen and the degree of damage or loss that may result.

Cybersecurity risks is the risk of loss of critical data or information, causing loss of control, loss of reputation, and loss of financial resources. There are different types of cybersecurity risk incidents, faced by organizations, which if occur cause the loss of data or information and resources.

Below are some of the significant cybersecurity risks types, which cause data and information losses:

Malware

Malware is malicious software such as spyware, ransomware, viruses, and worms. Malware is activated when a user clicks on a malicious link or attachment, which leads to installing dangerous software. Cisco reports that malware, once activated, can:

- Block access to key network components (ransomware)
- Install additional harmful software
- Covertly obtain information by transmitting data from the hard drive (spyware)
- Disrupt individual parts, making the system inoperable

Denial of Service

A denial of service (DoS) cyber-attack floods a computer or network and restrict the ability of systems to respond to requests. A distributed DoS (DDoS) does the same thing, but here the attack originates from a computer network. Hackers use a flood attack to disrupt the process, and they carry out a DoS.

Some cyber-attackers use the time that a network is disabled, to launch other attacks. A botnet is a type of DDoS in which millions of systems can be infected with malware and controlled by a hacker. Botnets target and overwhelm a target's processing capabilities. Botnets are hard to trace and are in different geographic locations.

Phishing

Phishing attack uses a fake email or communication, to trick the recipient into opening the email or communication message, and carrying out the instructions provided in such email or communication, such as providing a credit card number. The goal here is to steal the sensitive data, like the credit card and login information, or to install malware on the victim's machine to gain access to confidential information.

Password Attacks

With the use of right password, a cyber attacker may gain access to a file, or system to gain access to the data or information. Social-engineering is one of the types of password attack in which a strategy is used by the cyber attackers that relies heavily on human interaction, and may also involve tricking people into breaking standard data or information security controls. The other types of password attacks include accessing a password database of the organization or performing outright guessing.

Cyber Threat Targets, Impacts, and Activities

Cyber risk or cyber threat incident actors are involved in the performance of malicious activities against anything connected to or residing on the web including devices, information, and resources. Following are different factors which are considered, when organization need to assess the data and information security measures.

- Devices includes connected technology such as personal cell phones or computers, servers, and the operational technology that controls industrial processes. Once compromised, devices can be used to facilitate further cyber threat activity.

- Information includes intellectual property, other sensitive business information, and personal information. This could also include valuable financial information such as banking details or logins.

- Resources include assets such as fiat currency and digital assets, including cryptocurrency. Cyber threat actors often target Canadian individuals with fraud and scams aimed at convincing victims to send money to a threat actor to avoid a punishment or receive a fictional reward. Cyber threat activity aimed at financial institutions and systems may intend to steal much larger sums.

- Opinions can be influenced and reputation of the organization which can be damaged through the online malicious activities, such as disinformation, misinformation, or mal information.

Cyber or information security threat incident actors may target the stakeholders, individuals, or social discourse more broadly, by influencing specific events.

Identifying Cyber Threat Activity

Attribution is an act of determining accurately the cyber threat actor who is responsible for a particular set of cyber-attack related activities. Successful attribution of a cyber threat actor is important for different purposes, including the defense of network, law enforcement, foreign relations, and the deterrence. Attribution can be difficult as many cyber threat actors attempt to evade it through obfuscating their activities.

Obfuscation includes the techniques that cyber threat actors use to hide their true identities, techniques used, and their personal financial or other objectives. To avoid leaving clues that defenders could use to attribute the activity, threat actors may also use different special tools that covertly send information over the web.

Sophisticated threat actors may conduct the false flag operations, where the actor mimics the known activities of other actors with the hope of causing defenders to falsely attribute the activity to someone else. A nation-state could use a tool believed to be used extensively by cybercriminals or other nation-states in the hopes that it will be attributed to them.

The ability of cyber threat actors to obfuscate their activities varies according to the level of sophistication, and their motivation. In general, the competent cybercriminals are more adept at obfuscation than other cyber threat actors.

CHAPTER 21

Information Security Risk Management Process

What is Risk, and Risk Management

Risk is the function of the likelihood of a given negative incident resulting in adverse event for the organization. Risk is seen as a negative event, however all the risks are not negative, such as the risk taken by an organization to enter into a new market or risk taken to launch a new product. Organizations face risks because of the nature and type of the business activities, they undertake. Organizations set the risk appetite level to ensure that the level is not breached, and business or operational activities are performed considering the level set for taking risks.

Organizations also face different threats, and system vulnerabilities.

A threat is a potential for a particular threat-source, to successfully exercise the vulnerability causing harm and losses to the data or information system.

In the process of assessing threat-sources, the important element to be considered by the organizations include considering all the potential and possible threat-sources, which could cause losses or harm to the IT systems and resources, and the processing ability of such systems.

Although the data or information threat statement for an IT system located in a remote location, such as the desert may not include natural flood, because of the very low likelihood of such an event's occurring.

Environmental threats such as a bursting pipe may quickly flood the system or computer rooms and may cause significant damages to the organization's IT systems and resources.

A vulnerability is the weakness which can be accidentally triggered or it can be intentionally exploited.

Characterizing data and systems enables setting the scope of the risk assessment process, and it delineates the operational authorization and set the boundaries for the assessment of risks. It provides information related to hardware, software, system connectivity, and responsible division or support personnel, which is essential to define and assess the existing and potential risks.

Risk management encompasses the identification, analysis, and response to risk factors that form part of the life of a business. Effective risk management means attempting to control, as much as possible, future outcomes by acting proactively rather than reactively. Therefore, effective risk management offers the potential to reduce both the possibility of a risk occurring and its potential impact. Risk management structures are tailored to do more than just point out existing risks. A good risk management structure should also calculate the uncertainties and predict their influence on a business. Consequently, the result is a choice between accepting risks or rejecting them. Acceptance or rejection of risks is dependent on the level of tolerance that a business has already defined for itself.

If a business sets up risk management as a disciplined and continuous process for the purpose of identifying and resolving risks, then the risk management structures can be used to support other risk mitigation systems. It includes planning, cost control, organizing, and budgeting. Risk management process empowers the organization with the necessary tools, so that it can identify and deal with risks. Once risks are identified, it becomes easier for the organization to mitigate it. Further, the risk management process provides the organization with a basis on which it can undertake appropriate strategic and operational decisions.

For an organization, assessment, and management of different types of risks is the way to prepare for eventualities that may come in the way of progress and growth. When an organization evaluates its plan for handling potential threats and then develops structures to address them, it improves its odds of becoming a successful entity. The progressive risk management ensures risks of a high priority are dealt with aggressively. Further, the management will have the necessary information that they may use to make the informed decisions, and ensure that the organization remains secured.

Risk analysis is a qualitative problem-solving approach that uses various tools of assessment to work out and rank risks for the purpose of assessing and resolving them. Here is the risk analysis process:

Risk identification involves the process of brainstorming, where the organization gathers its employees together, to review all the various sources of risk. The next step is to arrange all identified risks based on priority. Because it is not possible to mitigate all existing risks, prioritization ensures that those risks that can affect a business significantly are dealt with more urgently.

The problem resolution involves identifying the problem and then finding an appropriate solution. However, prior to figuring out how best to handle risks, a business should locate the cause of the risks by asking the question, "What caused such a risk and how could it influence the business?"

Once an organization is set on assessing likely remedies to mitigate identified risks and prevent their recurrence, it needs to ask the following questions: What measures can be taken to prevent the identified risk from recurring? In addition, what is the best thing to do if it does recur?

Here, the ideas that were found to be useful in mitigating risks are developed into several tasks and then into contingency plans that can be deployed in the future. If risks occur, the plans can be put to action.

Information Security Risk Management Practices

An effective approach of risk management process is one of the important components of a successful IT security framework. The principal goal of risk management process should be to protect the organization and its ability to perform their mission, not just its information technology assets or IT resources. Therefore, the appropriate risk management process should not be considered or treated as a technical function carried out by the people who are IT experts, operating and managing the IT system, but as an essential management function of the organization. Information Security risk is the negative impact of the exercise of a vulnerability, considering both the probability and the impact of occurrence.

Risk management is the process of identifying risk, assessing risk, and taking steps to reduce risk to an acceptable level. This guide provides a foundation for the development of an effective risk management program, containing both the definitions and the practical guidance necessary for assessing and mitigating risks identified within IT systems. The ultimate goal is to help organizations to better manage IT-related mission risks.

The objective of risk management process should be to enable the organization to achieve its objectives and strategic mission through the use of better IT systems that store, process, or transmit critical information. Appropriate risk management process enables management to make well-informed risk management decisions to justify the expenditures that are part of the IT budget. By assisting the senior management and the IT team supports the documentation, resulting from the performance of risk management.

For an effective risk management practices, the following need to be considered in the prescribed order:

Identification of Data or Information Systems Used

Every organization uses systems and processes as a first step, which is recommended because the organizations perform different operational and business activities which need consolidation and classification. System identification is a process which involves identification of implemented systems, and information assets, that provide support to the organization's business and operational activities.

The organizations should prioritize all the identified data sources and information systems with a relevant business value. The value assigned considers the criticality of the information system, in terms of the cost associated with such system or data source. Assigning business value considers factors including criticality of data or information system, and their use in making decisions.

Organizations may consider to assign the ownership to the data and information systems, for the identified data and information technology assets, with clear responsibilities to protect the data and information systems.

Risk identification involves review of the available and relevant documents, such as internal policies and procedures, legislative requirements, frameworks, directives, or standards. The system documentation may also be used for the identification of data or information related threats or risks.

IT risk management team uses the system user guide, administrative or instruction manual, system designs and requirement documents, and other data security-related documentation or manuals. The team may also use previous IT audit reports, risk assessment reports, system test results reports, data security plan, and other data security policies which may provide relevant risk information, and the data security controls implemented by the management. An organization's mission and objective statements analysis or the performance of asset criticality assessment, enables information regarding system and data criticality and sensitivity.

The use of scanning tools, which are proactive technical methods to be used for the collection of information for risk identification. For example, a network mapping tool may identify the services which run on a large group of hosts, and it provides a way to build the individual profiles of the IT systems, use for the identification of risks.

Steps Involved in Information Security (IS) Risk Management

Risk management is an ongoing process, and need to be performed in an appropriate and logical manner. Information security risk management process requires identification of risk sources, for assessment and evaluation of relevant information or data security risks.

The following steps are involved in the process of performing information security risk management. These steps are followed in sequence, by the information security risk management team, of an organization:

- Defining information security risk sources
- Information security risks identification
- Information security risk assessment
- Mapping of information security risks with controls
- Evaluation of information security controls operating effectiveness

Defining Risk Sources

There are different risk sources that are used by the information risk management team, to identify the information security or cybersecurity risks, faced by the data, information systems and other IT assets of the organization.

Some of the important sources of information security risks are as follows:

- Information or cybersecurity related laws and regulations
- Internal information or cybersecurity policies, processes and procedures
- Internal information security breaches or incidents recorded in internal loss databases
- Media news
- Possible threats of cyber-attack

Applicable cybersecurity or data protection laws and regulations, issued by the regulatory authorities, contain different provisions and sections, which organizations are required to understand and comply with, through the implementation of appropriate information security processes and internal controls. Non-compliance with applicable data protection or information security laws and regulations, is a compliance risk, and may lead to imposition of fines and penalties. Therefore, information security risks can also be identified from the applicable laws and regulations, for the performance of risk assessment.

Internal information security or cybersecurity policies and procedures, developed and implemented, need to be complied with by all the employees, to ensure that data or information sources are protected and not misused. Therefore, information security risks can also be identified from the internal policies and procedures, to map against the relevant data or information security controls.

Organizations need to maintain information or data loss incidents, which comprises of previously occurred losses or data breach incidents. Internal databases are used to assess the possibility of occurrence of same data or information security risks, which occurred earlier.

Risk Identification

Information security risks are identified from the information and data systems used or developed by the organization, to store the data or information. Information and data owners and custodians are the people, who possess the actual knowledge base of the customers, operations, and other business activities. Risks are also identified through the analysis of information security incidents database maintained. The information or data loss database includes past data loss incidents, cyberattack incidents, and other data misuse incidents identified and reported at different branches, offices, or locations of the organization. Such data or information loss database, need to be timely updated, to ensure that it is appropriately used by the information risk management team and other stakeholders, for the purpose of identification of existing data or information security risks.

External sources such as information received from the customers, such as customer complaints or inquiries may also indicate the possibility of information security risks, for the organization. All customer complaints should be identified and recorded as part of the customer complaints management system, and it should be used during the process of data or information security risks. Customers may complaint about the organization weak cybersecurity control or may highlight the potential vulnerability to the systems and resources.

Information security risks may also be identified through the analysis of regulatory breaches, and fines imposed by the regulators. Indicators of information security breaches also include the pressures on employees from the senior management, to meet the targets, causing unauthorized information and data disclosures or misuse. Regulatory bodies may enquire regarding the potential or particular fraud incident, which it also serves as the risk source for the organization. Such regulatory enquiries should be considered for the information security risk identification process.

Industry study and trends analysis may also indicate information security risks and data frauds, if the industry is growing in a particular area but the organization itself is struggling to grow. Senior management must analyze these trends, to identify existing or potential information security risks which are inherent in the processes and departments.

Data or information fraudsters are also considered for the risk identification. Fraudsters usually fall into different categories, including "pre-planned data fraudsters" who intend to commit fraud from the beginning and may be short-term fraudsters, such as those who use stolen credit cards to gain financial benefits or may use false social security numbers. Fraudsters may also be the Intermediate data fraudsters who in the beginning work as the honest employees or staff but turn to fraud when times get hard, such as they may get frustrated at being passed over for promotion or the need may need serious financial needs to run the family matters. Slippery-slope data fraudsters are the fraudsters who are simply involved in trading businesses objectively. They are not in a position to pay their debts to run the affairs of the business. All these types of fraudsters are considered in relation to possible data or information fraud incidents.

Risks need to be identified by the experienced people, who know about the data, information, processes, and information system functionalities. Usually, information security team is responsible to collaborate with different stakeholders, to identify and assess the data and information security risks, for assessment and evaluation. Different stakeholders are involved in the process of risk identification, and they give relevant information and evinces to support the risks identified. Risks identified are recorded in an appropriate manner, for analysis and assessment. Identified risks need to be tagged against the relevant risk categories, including the data or information security risks.

Risk Assessment Process

Risk assessment involves performing the inherent, and residual risks assessment considering the likelihood and impact of the identified information security risks and controls.

Risk Assessment and Re-assessment

Risk assessment is the first process in the risk management methodology. Organizations perform risk assessment, to determine the extent of the potential vulnerability or threat, and the risks associated with internal systems, data resources, and other IT system. In the assessment of risks related to the IT system, the first step is to define the scope of the effort, where the boundaries of the system and data resources are identified, along with the resources and the information that constitute the system.

Risk assessment should be performed which shall help the organization, to determine the potential threats, and vulnerabilities and their impacts and consequences, to the identified data and information systems. Information security risks needs to be assessed from all aspects of IT Security including physical, administrative, environmental, and technical aspects.

It should also identify the sources of threats and potential vulnerabilities, the likelihood of the occurrence of an event that will exploit that vulnerability and the resulting adverse impact of that event. Risk re-assessment should be a continuing process.

For the performance of risk assessment, the organization may consider various factors, such as past cyberattack incidents, the particular type of information security risk relevant to the industry, internal control environment, available data, or information resources to address data fraud, data fraud prevention controls, ethical standards followed, unexplained data losses, receipt of different customer complaints, etc. Based on general information security assessment and utilization of available information, the information security risk assessor develops or designs the preventive and detective controls in various processes, and activities of the organization.

The preventive and detective controls are mostly implemented in high-risk processes, which are those where chances of occurrence of information security incidents are high. Such processes include servers, networks, systems, applications, online service delivery channels, etc. Once the likelihood of information security risks are assessed, then the frequency of occurrence of the information security incidents are assessed. The frequency is assessed based on the availability of past or historical information about the information security incidents.

Controls Mapping and Mitigation

Internal controls are mapped with identified information security risks. Preventive controls are built and implemented, to prevent the occurrence of information security risk incident, whereas, detective controls are controls that detect the occurrence of information security incident or data breaches.

General controls are differentiated from the process-specific data or information security controls, to prevent the information security risks. General controls support the organization as a whole such as the establishment of IT department, to ensure that all departments use technology to perform their duties. The process-specific information security controls include use of passwords, firewalls to protect the networks, restricted access to the confidential data or information, etc. which are built into the technology infrastructure, to ensure that all cyberattacks and information losses are avoided.

Risk mitigation controls should be developed and implemented to mitigate the identified data or information security risks, and protect the organization's strategic mission at the appropriate cost, with minimal possible risk impact, to the purpose and objectives. The recommended procedural and technical data or information security controls should be evaluated, and prioritized considering the operational impact of the identified information security risks, feasibility of the relevant mitigation controls, and the cost-benefit analysis of the mitigation strategies and controls. Once, all the data and information security controls are mapped with identified data or information security risks, the weak controls are the identified and segregated.

On the identification of weak data or information security controls, the initiatives need to be taken by management, to design and establish robust information security controls, necessary to mitigate the identified data and information asset risks.

Performing Information Security Reviews

The sound information security compliance governance structure is the foundation of an effective security program, and it requires the board of directors and senior management to ensure that processes are designed and set to ensure that compliance breaches are not reported or occurred. Information and data monitoring involves monitoring of the defined rules, processes, and activities of the employees to ensure that data breaches are identified and reported to relevant authorities for corrective actions and management of compliance risks.

The monitoring activity checks the "tone at the top" as this is part of the risk management practices. To ensure appropriate oversight of the compliance culture, the Board of Directors forms a Board level sub-committee, to periodically monitor the compliance practices and measures taken by the management. The compliance monitoring activities ensure that the governance structure is well established and functioning appropriately.

Information Security monitoring involves the intervention of the Information Security Committee which, headed by the Chief Executive Officer of the organization. The committee works on behalf of the Board, to regularly review and provide appropriate feedback to the management and employees, regarding the overall information security risk profile of the organization. Committee being part of the overall governance structure serves to set the compliance tone within the organization and works through the Information Security team. The monitoring team performs the risk-based approach toward managing the Regulatory requirements and works to ensure that information security and cybersecurity policies and procedures are effectively implemented, in the organization. IT Security Practitioners such as the network, application, system and database administrators, the computer specialists, security analysts, or security consultants are responsible for the proper implementation of appropriate information security requirements in internal systems. Based on the occurrence of changes in the internal IT systems and processes such as the expansion in the network connectivity, changes to existing infrastructure and internal information or information technology policies, the IT security practitioners should provide necessary support or they should use the risk management process for the purpose of identifying and assessing new information security risks, and takes measures to implement new data or information security controls, needed to protect and safeguard the technology resources, such as internal IT systems.

Risk management process is the responsibility of management and employees working in the organization. The key roles of the employees should support, and participate in the process of information security risk management. Senior Management under the standard of due care, is responsible for the accomplishment of internal and corporate mission, and it must ensure that the necessary resources are effectively applied to develop the capabilities needed to accomplish the mission. Senior management and employees should assess and incorporate results of the risk assessment process into the decision-making process. An effective risk management program that assesses and mitigates IT-related mission risks requires the support of governance or senior management.

The Chief Information Officer (CIO) is responsible for the agency's IT planning, budgeting, and performance including its information security components. Decisions made in these areas should be based on an effective risk management program.

The System and Information Owners are responsible for ensuring that proper controls are in place to address integrity, confidentiality, and availability of the IT systems and data they own.

Typically, the system and information owners are responsible for changes to their IT systems. Thus, they usually have to approve and sign off on changes to their IT systems (e.g., system enhancement, major changes to the software and hardware). The system and information owners must therefore understand their role in the risk management process and fully support this process.

Information and data monitoring is a regular process being performed by the information security compliance team. Monitoring and continuous improvement in the information security infrastructure and controls, are the responsibility of the all employees and management of the organization. They are required to support the information security team, in the prevention and detection of cybersecurity threats and vulnerabilities. The information security team performs periodic data protection and information security related compliance reviews. Through identification of compliance risks, breaches, and incidents and recommending appropriate recommendations in the light of applicable regulations. Team helps management in the protection of data from breaches and losses and works to avoid the reputational and financial losses.

The monitoring team ensures that the organization is not involved in the wrong practices of performing the business operations, transactions, and use of technology solutions. Monitoring team ensures that the effective information security program is in place and approved by the Board, for employees' reference and compliance purposes. Monitoring involves checking whether the policies cover relevant information and data security related regulatory elements. Monitoring involves checking the transactions, networks, systems, employees' behaviour towards data access, and activities of the customers, and matching them with the information security program. Information security team monitors that the critical customers' data and information are identified and protected appropriately. Identified data breaches or cybersecurity attempts are monitored and escalated to senior management for review and necessary actions.

Conclusion

THROUGHOUT this book, we have explored the fundamental principles of risk assessment and management, empowering individuals, and organizations to make informed decisions and navigate the unpredictable nature of our world.

We began our journey by understanding the nature of risk itself, recognizing that risk is an inherent aspect of human existence and is present in every endeavor we undertake. By embracing a proactive approach to risk assessment, we have learned to identify and analyze potential risks, evaluating their likelihood and impact on our objectives. Armed with this knowledge, we have been able to make informed decisions and take calculated risks to achieve our desired outcomes.

The process of risk management has been thoroughly examined, emphasizing the importance of developing robust risk mitigation strategies. We have explored various techniques and tools that enable us to prioritize risks and allocate resources accordingly. By adopting a comprehensive risk management framework, we have been able to minimize vulnerabilities, enhance resilience, and seize opportunities that lie within risk.

Moreover, this book has emphasized the significance of fostering a risk-aware culture within organizations and society at large. By promoting open communication, collaboration, and learning from past experiences, we can create an environment where risks are identified early, reported without fear of repercussions, and managed effectively. Through shared responsibility and collective efforts, we can build a foundation for sustainable growth and success.

While no risk assessment or management system can guarantee absolute certainty or eliminate all risks, the knowledge and principles presented in this book equip us with the necessary tools to make well-informed decisions and minimize the negative impacts of uncertainties. By embracing risk as an opportunity for growth and innovation, we can transform challenges into stepping stones to success.

As we bring this book to a close, it is essential to remember that risk assessment and management are ongoing processes that require continuous evaluation, adaptation, and improvement. The dynamic nature of our world demands vigilance and flexibility in our approach to risk. By embracing a mindset of resilience and constantly honing our risk management skills, we can navigate the ever-changing landscape with confidence and seize the opportunities that await us.

Printed in the USA
CPSIA information can be obtained
at www.ICGtesting.com
LVHW061356271223
767140LV00058B/921